# A Temporary Matter

## A Comedy in Two Acts

## Caedon Venné

Space Cadets Studios

Edited by Brent Winzek

Cover art & design by Monica Kay

For more, visit spacecadetsstudios.com

ISBN: 979-8-9885955-8-8

# DEDICATION

For my family and friends, who show me unwavering support. For my theatrical inspirations, mentors, and peers, who inspire me to pursue what I love and *create*.

For Aubri, for making me a better person every day.

In memory of Toby Maykuth.

# ACKNOWLEDGMENTS

This work would not be possible without the keen authoring advice of Aubri McCune and Dan Stevens. They have helped in more ways than they know and vastly contributed to the development of this story.

The playwright would also like to acknowledge all who took part in the developmental process of this play: the fantastic actors of both table reads, Kelly Tunney for his photography, Jon Sape for his videography, the *Space Cadets Studios* team for everything, and the future creatives who will contribute to this story taking shape.

Lastly, the playwright would like to acknowledge publisher, editor, and good friend Brent Winzek for his ceaseless support, advice, and expertise. If it wasn't for Brent's willingness to donate his time to the project, the script likely would've sat unseen at the bottom of a hard drive. It is solely because of Brent that this story is now available to be read, seen, heard, and shared. More importantly, Brent inspired Caedon to keep writing, to continue telling stories, and to *always* follow his dreams.

*What a tremendously special gift to give.*

# CONCEPTUAL STATEMENT

My initial concept for *A Temporary Matter* came about during the latter years of my undergraduate program in the post-pandemic educational setting. Even after the pandemic had come to a close, every one of my required courses was online in some capacity; fully asynchronous, global online, or Interactive TV (report to a classroom and watch an online meeting), except for my only elective... *choir*. My degree was coming from a screen, even after we 'recovered' from the pandemic; what many believed would be a temporary readjustment changed *everything*, especially in the development of our education system. Through those years, I became increasingly dissatisfied with the state of my education and found I was not alone. I was then inspired to bring this play to light in *all* its absurdity with the belief that laughter and reflection would lead to *hope*.

I believe that, paradoxically, technology has jumpstarted efficient communication, but severely damaged people's communication *skills*. This is what *A Temporary Matter* is centered on: communication, learning, and cooperation through a screen... and the difficulties, irregularities, and absurdities that follow.

*— Caedon Venné*

# PERFORMANCE RIGHTS

# PRODUCTION HISTORY

## FIRST TABLE READ

The initial reading of *A Temporary Matter* took place on March 14th, 2025, with *University Players* at *Pennsylvania Western University (California)*, with the following cast:

PROFESSOR ............................................Aubri McCune
HUSBAND.................................................... Blake Dowd
GILBERT ......................................Quenten Zboyovsky
VIOLA................................... Amelia Passarelli-Roberts
GREGORY ......................................... Eddie Guadalupe
KYLE................................................... Elijah Grier
MALLORY ................................................ Emily Bittner
ZACK ....................................................Seth Springsteen
BRI ...........................................................McKinley Klotz

## SECOND TABLE READ

The second read for *A Temporary Matter*, produced by *Space Cadets Studios*, took place on August 10th, 2025, with the following cast:

PROFESSOR ............................................ Cait Crowley
HUSBAND....................................................Paul Guyet
GILBERT ......................................K'nique Eichelberger
VIOLA............................................ Mia Moser
GREGORY ......................................Joe Kosha
KYLE...........................................Larry Robert Smith III
MALLORY ................................................Trisha Holmes
ZACK ...................................................... Noah Kendall
BRI ................................ Emma Elizabeth Thorpe Jones
STAGE DIRECTIONS .........................Aubri McCune

# CONTENTS

# CHARACTERS

**PROFESSOR** – (F) late 20s or early 30s, an anxious first-time adjunct professor with poor technology skills and a tenuous marriage.

**HUSBAND** – (M) late 20s or early 30s, an erratic and overworked IT technician, pants-off enthusiast, and classical music "performer." Maritally defiant.

(KYLE) **GILBERT** – (M/N) 18, a shithead student amidst an identity crisis. There's nothing he can't get away with... *probably.*

**VIOLA** – (F/N) 18, a successful Type-A student with the short end of the stick. She'd have decent leadership skills if she wasn't so quiet.

**GREGORY** – (M/N) 18, an overly-cautious germaphobe caught in the false media trap of Facebüch. Hardcore stubborn, very m'lady.

**KYLE** (GREGORY) – (M/N) 20, hopelessly "in love" with Mallory. Unexpectedly wise. Proud member of the *Kyle Club*.

**MALLORY** – (F/N) 18, hopelessly "in love" with Kyle. Pretty pink girl's girl. Realizes she's never been independent: cue transformative journey.

**ZACK** – (M/N) 19, sleeps the whole time. Ends up the most observant of the bunch. Also plays **THERAPIST**, (Gilbert's) **MOM, IT ZACHARY,** and **CIO.**

**BRI** – (F/N) 18, chronically late. Takes a liking to Husband. Also plays **HR BRIANNA**, and (Gregory's) **DAD.**

# PRODUCTION NOTES

**PLACE:** Many various chunks of space pulled from individual characters' homes, conjoined by the liminal space of technology.

**DIVERSITY, EQUITY, & INCLUSION:** Each character in this play can and should be played by any individual of any race, ethnicity, gender identity, sexuality, or body type. The more diversity the better. Next to each character description, there is F, M, or N listed. These are not rules to follow, but guidelines based on what was originally intended while writing. The script should be adjusted to reflect the casting choices.

*For more, see* "Notes for the Director" *in the Appendix.*

# PRESHOW

*Early morning—sometime in the 2020s—during a national lockdown.*

*Nine different desk arrangements are separated into tiles of space, grid-like. They are clearly from various locations in the real world, and are not school desks, but private spaces with the clutter, decorations, and personalization of each character. The desks sit alone in the dark, aside from one isolated in spotlight:* PROFESSOR*'s.*

*A vast projector screen looms in the background. It is disconnected from the real world (i.e. the characters cannot see it) and is currently projecting the screen saver of Professor's open computer: a slideshow of her photo album with* HUSBAND. *Smiling. Laughing. Love. Some suggestions:*

*Their first date, anniversaries, and birthdays.*
*Moving in together.*
*Game nights and parties.*
*Vacations and adventures.*
*Buying a car, a house, or a pet.*
*Husband's proposal…*

*And most importantly, their wedding day.*

*The screensaver cycles through numerous old photos of happy times. Soon, the house lights dim, and after a beat, the projector screen fades to the empty darkness of dormancy.*

LIGHTS DOWN

# ACT I, SCENE 1
## MARRIAGE COUNSELING

SFX: HALLELUJAH CHORUS

*G.F. Handel's* Hallelujah Chorus *plays. The first three bars pass, and* "**A TEMPORARY MATTER**" *flashes onto the screen as the choir sings their first "Hallelujah." A few measures play before the music is abruptly stopped by:*

*Screen and stage to total* BLACKOUT

SFX: STATIC

*A long beat of static silence passes between worlds before:*

SFX: LOG ON

*The screen lights up with the live projection of an online meeting. A sterile white spotlight falls on* THERAPIST's *tile; he begrudgingly flips through a script.*

SFX: LOG ON

*Spotlight on Husband's tile as he joins the meeting. He is pants-less, sporting a white tank top. He looks a bit anxious as he fiddles with his keyboard, trying to change his name, which is currently "Dickwad." Therapist genuinely thinks this is Husband's name and pronounces it* dih-QUAD, *as others will do later.*

THERAPIST: Hello. (*beat*) Hello? Mr. Dickwad?

SFX: LOG ON

*Spotlight on Professor's tile as she joins the meeting, dressed ultra professionally. She clicks around frantically.*

THERAPIST: Hello? Can you hear me? (*beat, silence*) Fuckin' thing.

*Therapist smacks his computer around; adlib it up. Smack! Smack! Shake... He hits the computer one last time, and:*

BLACKOUT

SFX: RUMBLING

*They are transported through the liminal space of technology, through memories, and through time. Therapist exits as Professor and Husband are shunted to their starting positions in the events of... that day... Therapist addresses them in an omniscient voice, coming from everywhere and... nowhere? The rumbling fades into the background.*

THERAPIST: (*voice from beyond, coldly reading from a script*) Welcome to 'Brighter Days' Counseling and Social Services... (*under his breath*) Trademark pending. (*unenthusiastic*) Thank you for joining me. This step can be a difficult one to take, but the fact that you took that step shows a need for change. A drive to mend what was broken—

HUSBAND: I don't think anything's *broken*—

THERAPIST: (*voice from beyond*) Hold on, Mr. Dickwad.

HUSBAND: That's actually not my name—

THERAPIST: (*without acknowledgement*) Tell me about that day. The day that prompted you to seek my help. The day you realized your love was in jeopardy. The day... of *reckoning*...

*Beat. They are stifled to awkward silence, before:*

5

THERAPIST: (*voice from beyond, now meek*) Uh– that's all that's in the script. So... whenever you're ready, I guess.

SFX: RUMBLING

HUSBAND: (*beat*) Do you wanna tell it? It's kinda your story. I mean I'm a big part of it, but–

*The rumbling crescendos, before... silence.*

PROFESSOR: Sure.

SFX: EMAIL RECIEVED

LIGHTS UP

*Spotlight on Professor's tile. The projector screen glows to life with a live view of her computer. She instantly drops into the story, preparing nervously, holding a cup of coffee in one hand and a thick packet of papers in the other. Lights rise in the background, revealing Husband brushing his teeth. From this point on, pacing is key; emphasize chaos and rapidity.*

PROFESSOR: Okay. (*beat*) 'A Temporary Matter' is–

HUSBAND: (*muffled with toothpaste*) Hey! Big meeting today!

PROFESSOR: (*delightfully surprised*) I was just going over my stuff– I'm surprised you remembered!

HUSBAND: (*beat, spits toothpaste*) You have a meeting?

PROFESSOR: I told you last night–

HUSBAND: Shit– I'm sorry, hon. All I can think about is mine; I think– *think* I'm getting promoted after all this fucking work. Movin' up in the IT world, baby! Kickin' names, and… (*beat, confused*) whatnot.

PROFESSOR: Oh. (*beat*) Congrats–

HUSBAND: *And* promotions come with raises, ya know! Well, I mean– you *wouldn't* know, but– God! How much is it gonna be? Ten percent? Twenty percent? (*beat, suddenly anxious*) Christ… I gotta get hyped up! You don't mind, do you?

PROFESSOR: I [*actually do mind*]–

HUSBAND: Love ya!

*Husband has already exited to their bedroom and shut the door by the time Professor is able to respond.*

PROFESSOR: (*beat, dry*) Love you. (*aside to the audience*) We've been kinda busy for the last… while. He's been working overtime so I could finish grad school. But I was *just* hired as an adjunct professor, and that day, I was getting ready for my very first lecture. And while I'm trying to focus, he's in his own little world, bragging about this stupid promotion, interrupting me a million times– then he did what he *always* does to 'hype himself up.'

*Professor returns to the scene, frantically prepping, before:*

## SFX: HALLELUJAH CHORUS[1]

*The* Hallelujah Chorus *blasts from a Bluetooth speaker in Husband's room. Professor loses her place.*

PROFESSOR: *(under her breath)* Christ, that fucking song. *(practicing)* 'A Temporary Matter' is a–

*Husband dramatically bursts through the door, rocking out to the* Hallelujah Chorus. *He has thrown on a dress shirt, which he buttons as he crosses to the kitchen. He grabs a banana and chomps while he sings.*

HUSBAND: *(sung)*[2] For the Lord, God, omnipotent reigneth! Hallelujah! Hallelujah! hallelujah! hallelujah!

*Amidst the "hallelujahs," Husband exits back to the bedroom and slams the door behind him. The song and Husband's "singing" are still faintly audible.*

PROFESSOR: *(fourth wall)* You see how that can be annoying, right?

THERAPIST: *(voice from beyond)* Objectively!

PROFESSOR: *(returns to the scene)* Uh– *(practicing)* 'A Temporary Matter' is a short story– *(beat)* well, maybe I should set up the meeting. Uh–

*Husband bursts through the door again, still rocking out. He has thrown a tech-themed tie around his neck. He crosses to Professor's desk and snatches a pen.*

---

[1] To help the flow of the music and lines, footnotes have been used to denote what measure the lines occur at. This is M. 1.
[2] M. 12.

8

HUSBAND: (*sung*)[3] For the Lord, God, omnipotent reigneth! Hallelujah! Hallelujah! hallelujah! hallelujah!

*Amidst the "hallelujahs," Husband exits back to the bedroom and slams the door yet again. The song and Husband's 'singing' are still (unfortunately) audible.*

PROFESSOR: (*fourth wall*) So, knowing my husband, I knew he would just *have* to burst in *one more time.*

*A long beat passes before Husband bursts in once more, still rocking out, now more theatrical than before. He saunters over to Professor and plants a fat kiss on her face mid-song.*

HUSBAND: (*sung*)[4] The kingdom of this world– [*is become the Kingdom of our Lord and of His Christ...*].

PROFESSOR: (*shouted over music*) Can you turn that off!

HUSBAND: Oh! Sure! (*turns the music off*) What's up?

PROFESSOR: You need to join my meeting.

HUSBAND: Why?

PROFESSOR: I'm worried it won't work– Can you just, I dunno, IT test it?

HUSBAND: IT test? (*chuckles*) Uh– (*checks watch*) I'm a bit too busy for an IT test right now. How 'bout after my promotion?

PROFESSOR: My class starts in, like, ten minutes.

HUSBAND: Honey– promotions are *really* important–

---

[3] M. 22. This line is with the sopranos; Husband sings in-octave.
[4] M. 34.

PROFESSOR: I just need your help.

HUSBAND: (*beat*) Alright, I'm here to save you. Again.

PROFESSOR: I don't think I need *saving*–

HUSBAND: Me to the rescue! Again. (*quickly; impressed with himself*) Send me the link.

PROFESSOR: What? How? I– (*beat*) Via email?

HUSBAND: (*beat*) Yes.

PROFESSOR: Oh. Sure. Alright. Here we go. Email.

HUSBAND: Do you want me to–

PROFESSOR: I got it! Pfft, just an email. One little click. (*beat*) Well, it'll be quicker if you do it–

HUSBAND: There it is. (*types and sends the email... click!*)

SFX: EMAIL SENT

HUSBAND: (*dramatically*) See you on the other side...

*Husband sprints to his computer in the other room. He sits down with a flair and logs in as Professor practices.*

SFX: EMAIL RECIEVED

PROFESSOR: (*practicing*) Yes, Kyle? *Sure!* I can answer that! 'A Temporary Matter' is a short story–

SFX: HALLELUJAH CHORUS[5]

*Husband plays the* Hallelujah Chorus... *again. It is much louder than before. Professor loses her place... again.*

---

[5] M. 1 again. From now on, lyrics are not written into the script. HUSBAND just sings whenever he can... and I mean *whenever*.

PROFESSOR: Uh, where... shit. (*reading*) Author Jhumpa Lahiri focuses– (*louder*) focuses on the difficulties of communication– (*louder still*) between a married couple– (*even louder*) who use nightly power outages to fix their relationship– (*maximum volume*) by sharing secrets in the dark!

SFX: LOG ON

*Husband joins the call, checking himself out in the camera. He glimpses the Diana Damrau 'Queen of the Night' costume from* The Magic Flute *displayed on his wall and gets sidetracked. Music blasts through the Bluetooth speaker and the video call.*

HUSBAND: (*shouted*) Hey!

PROFESSOR: (*shouted, cannot hear him*) What?

HUSBAND: (*shouted*) You think I can still fit into the Queen of the Night?

PROFESSOR: (*shouted*) I can't hear you!

HUSBAND: (*shouted*) I just haven't worn it in *forever*–

PROFESSOR: (*shouted*) I can't *hear* you!

HUSBAND: (*shouted*) Oh! Why didn't you *say* so? (*turns off music*) Hallelujah! Right? (*beat*) Right? (*beat*) Uh– (*looks around*) everything looks good. You pass the IT test! Now check *this* out.

*Husband changes his background to the Grand Canyon.*

PROFESSOR: How did you–

HUSBAND: Wo-ho-*hoah*! FanTAStic view up here!

PROFESSOR: (*smiling*) I only have a few minutes–

HUSBAND: Look at the size of that *gorge!* Such a vast chasm of… *rocks*. If my measurements are correct, it's– WOAH! It's *nearly* as wide as–

PROFESSOR: *(sharply)* Don't make a vagina joke.

HUSBAND: *(beat, shocked)* –as… as *the!* The… distance! *Distance!* Between, uh, between– between me and– and *(beat… an idea) you.* Yeah. I just feel… far away from you right now. Yeah.

PROFESSOR: *(mocking)* You feel a *distance* between us?

HUSBAND: Mhm, mhm. *Yeah.* You're in a sad living room. I'm at the Grand-fucking-Canyon. Distance.

PROFESSOR: *(beat)* You were making a vagina joke.

HUSBAND: Yes, yes I was. *(beat)* Yup. I'll just, uh… change it back now. *(changes background to normal, changes his name to "Dickwad")* Look! Retribution!

THERAPIST: *(voice from beyond)* Ah, dickwad! That makes sense.

HUSBAND: *(beat)* Maybe I'll leave– I should leave.

SFX: LOG OFF

PROFESSOR: *(fourth wall)* Then, he made his best attempt at "comforting" me.

HUSBAND: You okay? Usually, you're not so touchy. I mean you're a *little* touchy but not *this* touchy.

*Professor scowls.* KYLE GILBERT *crosses to his tile in the dark. He sits, opening his laptop to log in for class.*

HUSBAND: (*cont.*) Listen, just *relax*. You're always so *stressed*. What are you even stressed about? We have meetings online all the time– I have mine in like twenty minutes– the one for my promotion! God, I can't *wait* to hear how much more I'm gonna make, like ten percent? Twenty percent? *Thirty* percent–

PROFESSOR: I only have a few minutes–

HUSBAND: Oh, right! Sorry, I was saying that… they… I… (*beat*) I forget what I was saying.

PROFESSOR: It was before you started talking about yourself.

HUSBAND: Oh! About my promotion? Yeah! Like will the raise be ten percent? *Twenty* percent? *Thir*–

PROFESSOR: No! No, you… have meetings online? All the time?

HUSBAND: Ah! Yes! They aren't that different from in-person. (*genuinely trying to comfort… failing*) The big difference is that you're online rather than… not. Honestly, it makes some things better– or *easier* I should say. Like I just sleep the whole time! I'm *sure* it'll be the same with teaching.

PROFESSOR: Sure. *Exactly* the same–

HUSBAND: Plus, when you're on a call, you don't have to wear pants. Bonus!

SFX: LOG ON

*Kyle Gilbert logs into class. He's early, and Professor doesn't notice him. A spotlight illuminates his workspace.*

13

PROFESSOR: You absolutely *do* have to wear pants.

HUSBAND: Uh, no you don't. Did you see my lower half at the Grand Canyon?

PROFESSOR: No, but that doesn't mean—

HUSBAND: See?! You don't need pants!

PROFESSOR: (*beat*) Yes, you do.

HUSBAND: No, you don't.

PROFESSOR: Yes, you do!

HUSBAND: No, you don't!

PROFESSOR: Yes you do!!!

HUSBAND: (*overlapping*) No—

KYLE GILBERT: (*overlapping*) No, you don't.

*Husband sprints out of the room, realizing his on-camera pants-less-ness. Professor leaps out of her chair to hide him.*

PROFESSOR: (*overlapping*) Shit— *shoot!* Sorry! Don't look! Sorry— I am so, so sorry!

HUSBAND: (*overlapping*) FUCK, FUCK, FUCK, FUCK, FUCK, FUCK, FUCK, FUCK, (*etc.*).

*Amidst the chaos, VIOLA enters in the darkness, happily strolls over to her tile, sits, and logs into class.*

PROFESSOR: I didn't see that you joined—

KYLE GILBERT: No, it's cool. Check it.

*He stands, presenting his pants-less-ness to the camera.*

PROFESSOR: (*shielding her eyes*) No! Please—

SFX: LOG ON

*Viola, logs into class early, just in time to behold Kyle Gilbert's pants-less-ness. On the SFX, her tile lights up. Generally, the lighting should mirror the individuals' log-on status; from now on, this is implied.*

VIOLA: Hi, profe– (*gasp!*)

SFX: LOG OFF

*Viola gasps and instantaneously logs off. She contemplates the brief[6] events she just witnessed.*

PROFESSOR: No! It's not– shit– *shoot!* Okay, sit down, or– or put some pants on! Please.

KYLE GILBERT: It's just nature! It's not a big deal.

PROFESSOR: *Clearly–* (*surprises herself; she didn't mean to say that*) No, I didn't mean–

KYLE GILBERT: Woah! *Woah!!!* Small penis joke?! Was that a [*small penis joke?*]–

PROFESSOR: No? No! I was *saying* that *clearly* it *is* a big deal! It is a *huge* deal.

KYLE GILBERT: Oooooooh, *thanks*...

PROFESSOR: Okay, pants on. *Now.*

KYLE GILBERT: Fine. Fine!– If hiding perfectly good– *large!* If hiding perfectly *large* and *manly* human nature will ease your pain... *fine.*

PROFESSOR: Ease my pain?

KYLE GILBERT: Yeah. (*beat, feigning confusion*) Wait, you aren't in any pain at the moment?

---

[6] Get it?

PROFESSOR: I mean, just a migraine.

KYLE GILBERT: No-no-no… I *meant* from that big ol' stick up your ass.

PROFESSOR: *What!?*

KYLE GILBERT: *Ooh!* Mic drop!

PROFESSOR: What's your problem? (*to herself*) I need to report you—

KYLE GILBERT: Pfft, try me! You don't even know who I am. You've only seen my face.

PROFESSOR: And now your crotch…

KYLE GILBERT: Yes! And my crotchular region— which you should thank me for— but you don't even know my name. You have *zero* evidence. (*quick*) Unless you're recording the meeting— are you recording the meeting?

PROFESSOR: Couldn't tell you if I was.

KYLE GILBERT: Then as far as I'm concerned, I'm in the clear.

PROFESSOR: (*leans in to read her screen*) "Kyle Gilbert?"

KYLE GILBERT: Oh *shit*—

SFX: LOG OFF

*Kyle Gilbert leaves the class. Husband sneaks in, still pants-less, now that the commotion has lulled.*

PROFESSOR: (*fourth wall*) I don't know about you, but I don't think there's ever been a worse start to a semester.

HUSBAND: (*responding in-scene*) It hasn't even *started* yet. It's five 'til– did he actually have a big pe[*nis*]–

PROFESSOR: (*not looking at him*) Can I have a favor?

HUSBAND: (*sigh*) Sure.

PROFESSOR: Can you please just, like, stay in a different room when my class starts? I know it's hard, stuck in here already. I– I *just* started this job and I feel *so close* to giving up.

HUSBAND: I think... Ya know what I think? I think that no one should *ever* give up. Especially not on their dreams.

*She turns, confused, to see him pants-less once again.*

PROFESSOR: Put some pants on.

*Husband frowns, turns sassily, and exits to the bedroom. Presumably to put on some pants. Presumably...*

PROFESSOR: (*shouted*) And can you grab me a glass of wine? This coffee is *not* waking me up.

HUSBAND: (*shouting back*) I don't think– (*quiet*) Okay.

PROFESSOR: (*fourth wall*) Then, the meeting crashed.

SFX: LOG OFF

PROFESSOR: (*furiously clicking random buttons*) What? What happened? (*shouted to the other room*) Uh, hey! I– (*beat*) No. No! I can... figure this out on my own. (*beat*) Help! Help! Help! (*cont.*)

*Husband sprints in from the other room, still pants-less, now wielding a fire extinguisher.*

17

HUSBAND: What! What! What's wrong?!

PROFESSOR: It crashed.

> GREGORY *enters in the dark and crosses to his desk. He persistently tries to log into the now-down class.*

HUSBAND: So you decided to *scream* for help?

PROFESSOR: I needed it, like, really bad.

THERAPIST: *(voice from beyond)* Okay, that was fucked up!

HUSBAND: *(in-scene)* I thought there was a fire! Or… *(beat)* I thought it was a fire.

PROFESSOR: No fire… But I *do* know a lady who needs you to put that degree to good use, Mr. Sexy… IT *(beat)* man…

HUSBAND: Well… if you put it like *that*. *(strikes a "sexy" pose)* BAM! *(presses a button, the call reopens)*

> SFX: LOG ON

PROFESSOR: How the fuck did you do that? What— *(beat)* I don't even wannna know.

HUSBAND: And you don't *need* to know. That's what I'm here for. *(plants a kiss on her forehead, turns)*

PROFESSOR: Awww! Now go put pants on. And grab me that wine!

> *Husband stops in his tracks. He slowly swivels back to her.*

HUSBAND: *No…*

PROFESSOR: *(beat)* No?

HUSBAND: *(beat, sassily defiant)* No.

PROFESSOR: No to *what*?

HUSBAND: The pants!

PROFESSOR: Why?!

HUSBAND: I don't WANT to–

SFX: LOG ON

*Gregory manages to log into the class. Professor jolts up to block Husband sprinting off into the other room to hide.*

PROFESSOR: (*overlapping*) Shit– *shoot!* Run! Run!

HUSBAND: (*overlapping*) FUCK, FUCK, FUCK, FUCK, FUCK, FUCK, FUCK, FUCK, (*etc.*).

*Professor puts on a fake smile as Gregory connects. He turns his camera on, wearing a heavy-duty mask.*

GREGORY: (*muffled behind a mask*) G'morning m'lady, good to see the conference has returnéd!

PROFESSOR: He-heyy, Gregory! Nice to [*see you*]–

*Gregory leaps out of his chair and scrambles back, six feet away, checking the distance with a tape measure.*

GREGORY: (*gasp!*) You aren't wearing a mask!

PROFESSOR: No, I'm home–

*Husband* Mission Impossible *army crawls into the kitchen to grab a glass of wine.*

GREGORY: Doesn't matter *where* you are, the spit particles– *sparticles*, if you will– travel through electricity... a process known as *Covidelectrosmosis*. Saw it on Facebüch. And *you* are not wearing a mask therefore I must remain six feet of distance to avoid your sparticles!

19

PROFESSOR: Sorry! I didn't hear about Spartacus—

*Professor confusedly searches for a mask. Gregory sees her in full professional attire and is taken aback.*

GREGORY: Wait, what are those?

PROFESSOR: (*looking around*) What's what?

GREGORY: Those *things* on your legs!

PROFESSOR: (*beat*) Pants?

GREGORY: You're wearing pants?

PROFESSOR: Okay— (*giving up her search for a mask*) I'm getting *really* tired of this pants shit.

*Professor crosses back to her desk. Gregory reacts, flailing his measuring tape like a whip.*

GREGORY: Woah! *Woah!!!* Not an *inch* closer! Sparticles! *Sparticles!!!*

PROFESSOR: What do you need! Why are you early!

GREGORY: Madame professor m'lady; Perchance I surreptitiously clicked 'join meeting.'

PROFESSOR: Great. See ya in five.

SFX: LOG OFF

*Professor miraculously kicks Gregory from the call. Husband enters cautiously, still pants-less, now with a glass of wine.*

HUSBAND: Is he gone?

PROFESSOR: Yes, thank God— (*beat*) You're *still* not wearing pants.

HUSBAND: I don't wanna wear pants! They're unnecessary!

PROFESSOR: What about my job makes it seem like pants are unnecessary? I'm trying to teach–

HUSBAND: Through a screen. A screen that can only see the top portion of your body, hence the pants-less-ness.

PROFESSOR: Oh my *god*–

*Viola has now worked up the courage to rejoin the class, just as Husband stands in the background without pants.*

HUSBAND: Plus, don't even *try* to tell me you don't like what you see!

*Husband begins doing some semi-erotic playful dance or gesture, first to the amusement, then panic of Professor.*

SFX: LOG ON

VIOLA: (*cautiously*) Professor– (*gasp!*)

SFX: LOG OFF

*Viola immediately leaves the call. Beat. The other students filter into their workspaces and prepare to log on. Husband backs up, terrified.*

HUSBAND: I am so sorry, I–

PROFESSOR: (*unbridled fury*) PANTS, SHORTS, A KILT, YOUR STUPID COSTUME, I DON'T CARE WHAT IT IS BUT COVER YOUR PASTY LEGS!!!

*In music terms, Attacca! Immediate segue to the next scene.*

21

# ACT I, SCENE 2

## THE LECTURE

*The full class is logged in, now onstage in their respective tiles. No one has their video on. A spotlight isolates Professor's tile. She instantly switches into 'teacher-mode.'*

PROFESSOR: (*sweetly, fake*) Hel-*lo* class! Welcome! (*beat, she looks around and sees no faces*) I would like to possibly see everyone's bright and shining faces! So, could we all turn our cameras on? (*silence*) How else can I put faces to names! Right? (*silence*) Right guys? (*silence*) Can... can anyone hear me? (*silence*) Is my microphone on?

SFX: CHAT NOTIFICATION

*Kyle Gilbert responds in chat. The text flashes onto the screen and should do the same for other "in chat" moments.*

KYLE GILBERT: (*in chat*) yes

PROFESSOR: (*annoyed*) Alright, uh– the syllabus. Oh, look at that! *Ahem*– Attendance is mandatory, and to be present, a student *must* have their camera on. (*silence*) And attendance will be... (*thinks*) ten percent of your grade.

*Lights up on Viola; she instantly turns her camera on.*

PROFESSOR: (*beat*) Just Viola? Okay... Oh wait! I *totally* misread that, sorry. Attendance will be *fifty* percent of your grade.

*Suddenly, everyone else turns their cameras on except for Kyle Gilbert and ZACK. Lights up on the whole stage, except for Kyle Gilbert, Zack, and BRI's dark corners.*

PROFESSOR: Great. Let's get started—

KYLE GILBERT: Your syllabus don't say any of that.

*Cameras off. Lights out again; only Professor is lit.*

PROFESSOR: It's an amendment.

*Cameras on except for Kyle Gilbert and Zack. Lights up on the whole stage, except for Kyle Gilbert, Zack, and Bri.*

KYLE GILBERT: You can't make amendments.

*Cameras off. Lights out again, only Professor is lit.*

PROFESSOR: *(accidentally rapping)* The first amendment is that I can, in fact, make amendments. The second is, "Cameras on or no attendance."

MALLORY: *(overlapping)* That was *so* Hamilton-coded!

KYLE GREGORY: *(overlapping)* I feel like that's a paradox—

PROFESSOR: *(sped through)* And attendance is fifty percent of your grade!

*Finally, all cameras are on... except for Zack. Lights up on all except for Zack (sleeping) and Bri (missing).*

PROFESSOR: Wonderful. It's great to see all your... *(looks around, all are miserable)* bright and shining faces. I'm excited to be here, and I'm glad you are too. *(silence)* Uh, speaking of being here, let's take attendance. *(beat)* Kyle?

BOTH KYLES: Here.

PROFESSOR: Oh. That's a problem. Can, uh– Can one of you be Kyle G?

BOTH KYLES: Fine. *Wait–*

PROFESSOR: Shit– *shoot!* Uh, sorry. Gilbert and Gregory. Do either of you have nicknames?

KYLE GILBERT: Yeah, some people call me–

KYLE GREGORY: Mallory calls me 'Daddy.'

MALLORY: *Kyle!!!*

BOTH KYLES: What?!

PROFESSOR: Stop! No one is going to call you that. Not even Mallory.

MALLORY: What?! Why not–

KYLE GREGORY: *(to Professor)* Are you for *real* right now?

PROFESSOR: Yes, for real! *(beat, regroup)* Sorry Kyle, what were you saying?

KYLE GILBERT: *(overlapping)* Some people call me–

KYLE GREGORY: *(overlapping)* Mallory calls me 'Daddy.'

PROFESSOR and MALLORY: *Kyle!*

BOTH KYLES: What?!

PROFESSOR: Quiet! Kyle *Gilbert.* What were you saying?

KYLE GILBERT: *(beat)* … Huh?

PROFESSOR: About what some people call you?

24

KYLE GILBERT: Oh. (*chuckles*) You don't wanna know.

PROFESSOR: (*scoffs*) Whatever. Kyle Gilbert, you are now Gilbert. Kyle Gregory, you are Gregory.

(KYLE) GILBERT: Wha– I don't wanna be Gilbert!

*Gregory is still standing six feet away, pants-less. He raises his hand, which is now sporting a blue rubber glove.*

GREGORY: Uh, pardon me, m'lady professor, but–

PROFESSOR: Shit– *shoot!* Gregory. You're here. (*sigh*) Why wouldn't you be. Kyle Gilbert, you are Gilbert, and Kyle Gregory, you are just Kyle.

KYLE (GREGORY): Cool.

*Kyle Gregory raises a freakin' dope-ass salute in the form of the ASL "K." Mallory sighs, swooning.*

MALLORY: (*under her breath*) 'Cool…'

(KYLE) GILBERT: What, so *he* gets to be Kyle and I have to be called *Gilbert?*

PROFESSOR: (*back to attendance*) Gilbert?

GILBERT: Here. Is all this necessary? I don't on participating–

PROFESSOR: Stop. Speaking. (*beat*) Kyle?

KYLE: (*pointing at himself*) Gregory?

GREGORY: Huh?

PROFESSOR: No, the *new* Kyle–

KYLE: Oh! (*takes a moment to get 'cool'*) Aloha.

25

*Kyle raises a freakin' dope-ass salute in the form of the ASL "K." Mallory sighs again.*

MALLORY: (*sigh*) "Aloha…"

PROFESSOR: What was that? Sign language?

KYLE: Yeah.

PROFESSOR: You know sign language?

KYLE: Nah. Just the K.

PROFESSOR: (*beat*) Alright. Viola?

VIOLA: (*meekly*) Here.

PROFESSOR: Hey, uh– I just wanted to apologize for the, uh– (*searches for words*) complications earlier.

VIOLA: No, it's okay– it's fine! Yeah. (*beat*) Can we just… move on?

PROFESSOR: Yes! Sure! That's a– a *great* idea. Uh– (*beat, sigh*) Gregory?

*Gregory is still six feet away, arms crossed, still pants-less.*

GREGORY: Currently in attendance. Announcement: everyone *must* don their masks. Otherwise, I am forced to stay a minimum of six feet of distance to avoid the ingestion of your sparticles. (*silence*) Because Covid travels through electricity? (*silence*) He-*llo*??? Covidelectrosmosis? *Facebüch?*

PROFESSOR: Yes, uh– for everyone's *comfort*–

GREGORY: And for the world's safety!

PROFESSOR: (*beat*) Yes. For the world's safety–

GREGORY: To be responsible human beings!

PROFESSOR: (*beat*) Yes. To be responsible–

GREGORY: And to prevent the transmission of sparticles through Covidelectrosmosis!

PROFESSOR: *Gregory*! (*beat*) Stop. Just– Everyone find a mask, I guess–

*The next chunk is incredibly fast-paced, each line overlapping with the last, building until it explodes...*

KYLE: Isn't *Sparticle* a TV show?

MALLORY: Oh, Kyle–

PROFESSOR: I don't [*know*]–

GILBERT: No, Sparticles is a platformer–

VIOLA: Sparticle is short for 'superpartner' in particle physics–

KYLE: It's like a mystery–

GREGORY: No, it's a *spit*-particle: a Sparticle–

VIOLA: It sort of *is* a mystery–

PROFESSOR: We're getting really sidetracked–

KYLE: In the show there's only one Kyle (*salutes*)– Oh! There is a Kyl-*ie* though–

GREGORY: A sparticle is–

MALLORY: Kyle, you are *so* smart.

PROFESSOR: Can we please get back on track–

GILBERT: You jump around and kill stuff, but the floor is *invisible*–

GREGORY: A sparticle is–

KYLE: Everyone over fifteen mysteriously *vanishes*–

MALLORY: *So* mysterious–

PROFESSOR: Can we *please* stop–

GREGORY: *(shouted)* A sparticle is a spit particle transmitted by Covidelectr[*osmosis*]–

*Lights up on Zack, who screams into his microphone.*

ZACK: EVERYONE SHUT THE FUCK UP! I'M TRYING TO SLEEP!

*Long beat of stunned silence. Professor ignores the outburst.*

PROFESSOR: *(back to attendance)* Zack?

ZACK: Here, bitch.

*Again, no reaction; she moves on.*

PROFESSOR: Bri. *(silence)* Bri? *(silence)* Okay– Mallory?

MALLORY: Hiiiiii– Mrs. Professor, is it possible to move my video next to Kyle's?

GILBERT: Stay the hell away from me!

MALLORY: Ew, not you *Gilbert*. Cool Kyle!

*Mallory raises a malformed 'Kyle salute' in an ASL "V."*

KYLE: *(ala* Pokémon) *Kyle!*

*Kyle raises the dope-ass ASL "K."*

GILBERT: *(smiling)* Don't call me Gilbert! My name isn't Gilbert!

*Gilbert tries not to smile, but he does. Mallory clocks this.*

MALLORY: Ew, why are you smiling you weird freak–

GILBERT: I'm not smiling! I– I *never* smile– *you* smile!

PROFESSOR: Calm! Calm. (*beat*) Mallory, I have no clue if it's possible to move you around.

MALLORY: Okay, let me rephrase. Can you please *find out* how I can be next to my *boyfriend?*

PROFESSOR: How would I [*do that*]–

MALLORY: Can't you ask your boss?

PROFESSOR: (*sarcasm*) Sure, I'll stop the *entire* class to ask my supervisor how to put your videos next to each other.

MALLORY: Great! *Thank youuuuu–*

PROFESSOR: No– (*sigh*) that was sarcasm, Mallory.

MALLORY: Sooo, you're not gonna ask your boss?

PROFESSOR: No.

MALLORY: Well, what about your boss's boss? 'cause you're like at the bottom of the totem pole so there's definitely people you can talk to about this whole *situation.*

PROFESSOR: (*beat*) Thanks for... validating my career.

MALLORY: You're *so* welcome! It's– (*a deeply distressed sigh*) It's just hard. It's really, *really* hard to be this far away from each other.

KYLE: Yeah, especially with the lockdown.

GREGORY: (*under his breath*) That's how it's *supposed* to be.

VIOLA: Guys, she already said no! Can we listen to our professor now?

GILBERT: Aren't you guys, like, neighbors?

MALLORY: Yes, *Gilbert*, but there are two walls, a patch of grass, and a screen between us. You couldn't *possibly* understand.

KYLE: Yeah, and we haven't touched in two days, three hours, and twenty-seven minutes–

MALLORY: And our love language is physical touch.

KYLE: And kissing through the masks is *really* hard. But! If you just cut open the middle you can do all sorts a' things! Like [*tongue stuff*]–

PROFESSOR: Okay! Okay! Cutting you off there.

VIOLA: Your videos being next to each other will solve your touch depravity? Sounds pretty placebo–

KYLE: No! We are *very* touch deprived– Twenty-*eight* minutes– even metaphorical touch is rare.

GREGORY: (*under his breath*) You're going to kill everyone.

GILBERT: You're all actually *so* annoying.

MALLORY: *You're* so annoying, *Gilbert*–

KYLE: Yeah! You're not even a *Kyle* anymore!

*Kyle mocks Gilbert, waving the ASL "K" in his camera.*

MALLORY: Just because–

PROFESSOR: Why don't we stop arguing so we can–

MALLORY: (*to Professor*) I was speaking before you *fully* interrupted me! (*beat*) Gilbert. Just because you're doomed to be alone for the rest of your life doesn't mean you can take that out on us.

PROFESSOR: (*to herself*) How did I kick him out...

GILBERT: Mallory. *Fuck you–*

SFX: LOG OFF

*Professor kicks Gilbert and Mallory into a breakout room. Their tiles go dark.*

PROFESSOR: Ah, that's how. Alright class, they've earned themselves a timeout.

KYLE: Mallory!!! No! Noooo-hoo-hoooo-hoooooo!!! (*collapsing to his knees, weeping*) Twenty-*nine* minutes...

SFX: CHAT NOTIFICATIONS

ZACK: (*in chat*) dam
autocorrect
i meant damn

*Viola and Professor stare at Kyle with... pity?*

VIOLA: Wow. To be loved like that–

PROFESSOR: I know, right? That was– wow. (*beat*) I miss that kind of love.

*Husband enters in a fourth wall break, hearing what Professor had just said. The class freezes.*

HUSBAND: You don't think I love you like that?

PROFESSOR: Well–

HUSBAND: (*fourth wall*) Because I do. I might not show it in the "crying when you leave" way—

PROFESSOR: That's not the point—

HUSBAND: What *is?* Is your point that I made mistakes? That I fucked up?

PROFESSOR: The point is that you disregard my needs for your own.

HUSBAND: *Disregard* you? Did you forget how hard I've worked so you could get your master's? And I'm so, *so* proud of you, but I feel like I haven't really had a life. Like, work *became* my life. That's why, when I heard the news— (*beat*) It's not an excuse, but—

PROFESSOR: (*fourth wall, to Therapist*) Do *you* have anything to say? Any, I don't know, *advice?*

THERAPIST: (*beat, voice from beyond*) Let's hear his story!

*Husband and Professor lock eyes. She exits as Husband crosses to his room and gets ready... to dance.*

LIGHTS FADE

SFX: QUEEN OF THE NIGHT

# ACT I, SCENE 3
## THE PROMOTION

LIGHTS UP

*Husband dances to the Queen of the Night's Aria ("Der Hölle Rache") from* The Magic Flute, *passionately and pants-less-ly during his work call. The audience shouldn't know he is on a call until* HR BRIANNA *is revealed. This 'dance' can go on for a while. Husband stops the music and collapses.*

HUSBAND: *(gasping for breath)* See that? Did you see that? That's the *power* of no pants. The pure *freedom* of the world wide web. Who would wanna sit through boring-ass meetings in any other way? *(beat)* No offense.

*Lights rise on HR Brianna. She is professionally dressed (with no pants), sitting patiently on the other end of the call.*

HR BRIANNA: Oh, none taken.

HUSBAND: Good! Yeah. I can just sit here and not pay attention, pants-less might I add, and move on! And the best part– wanna know the best part? *(Beat. HR Brianna isn't paying attention. He continues.)* Peace in my own home. Peace. *(glares out to the other room, beat)* Peace is one word for it. *(beat)* Ya know, I've lost like twenty pounds since the lockdown. Yeah. Ya know why? It's cause I don't pass *thirty* McDonald's on the way home. Because the new 'way home' is 'close my laptop, and leap inside my bed with pure joy and wonder.' Notice, I didn't say 'take off my pants,' because they're already off! BAM! What could be more *perfect* than that? (*beat*) Why can't she understand? (*mocking*) "Put some pants on! Put some pants on! My fancy new job is more important than yours! I have a bigger salary than you! Your tiny little legs are white as snow!" (*beat*) I can't remember what she said exactly, but my legs aren't even that pale! I'd call them eggshell at most.

HR BRIANNA: Maybe ivory?

HUSBAND: She can't berate me like that! She *needs* me. She wouldn't be *having* her dumb class right now if it wasn't for me! She can't even send an email, but *I'm* shamed for not wanting to wear pants? When you can't even *see* the lower half— when the lower half is *invisible*?! Did she even *see* me at the Grand Canyon? (*scoffs*) Probably not! She was paying more attention to her stupid coffee cup than me. Alcoholic. (*beat*) When *does* she pay attention to me anymore? She's... always worried about this and stressed out about that, but never *this* (*gestures to himself*). Me. If you didn't understand.

HR BRIANNA: I understand, Mr. Dickwad.

*He doesn't catch that. He just appreciates a 'listening' ear.*

HUSBAND: Ya know, I'm glad *someone* does.

HR BRIANNA: Have you considered that she may be trying to spite you?

HUSBAND: Spite me? No. No, she doesn't have a spiteful bone in her body. (*a change*) She's kind. Passionate. A dreamer for sure.

HR BRIANNA: People change.

HUSBAND: (*beat, a realization*) Ya know what? People do change. Some for the better (*gestures to himself*). Some for the worse (*glares out to Professor*).

HR BRIANNA: Absolutely. Speaking of change, Mr. Dickwad, back to your future with the company.

HUSBAND: Ah, yes. Yes! Uh– sorry for my little tirade. (*reenacting*) "Pants! No pants! Pasty little white legs!" Anyway, I was hoping– (*realization*) wait...

HR BRIANNA: Is there an issue?

HUSBAND: No. No! No issue, just... Did you just call me Mr. Dickwad?

HR BRIANNA: Yes?

HUSBAND: Ironically or unironically?

HR BRIANNA: *Un*-ironically. Is that not your name?

HUSBAND: No. (*a beat; he chuckles at himself*) That was a joke from earlier. Which normally would have made me look like an idiot if you didn't *actually* think that was my name. Now...

HR BRIANNA: Now what, Mr. Dickwad?

HUSBAND: (*beat*) In the years I've worked here, with you as my supervisor... you never learned my name. (*beat, another realization*) I was a number to you... (*overly dramatic, seething more with every word*) A tool to do your bidding, conforming to your twisted standards, and complying with every whim and wildly fanciful request– nay, demand! Every *demand* that spilled from your slimy little corporate coffee-stained alcoholic mouth!

HR BRIANNA: (*checks notepad*) Sounds about right.

HUSBAND: I quit. Fuck your two weeks' notice.

HR BRIANNA: Oh, that's wonderful! We were letting you go anyway. The pandemic has severely [*affected our budget*]–

HUSBAND: Wait! With severance pay?

HR BRIANNA: Absolutely.

HUSBAND: ... *How much?*

HR BRIANNA: (*beat*) Lots.

HUSBAND: No–no–no you can fire me! I'd much rather have severance pay than my dignity.

HR BRIANNA: Too late. You quit.

HUSBAND: We can't, like, backtrack?

HR BRIANNA: Let me check. (*checks her notepad*) No.

HUSBAND: Rewind?

HR BRIANNA: (*checks her notepad*) No. (*Husband takes a breath to speak*) No. In addition, Mr. Dickwad, we'll need you to join our next meeting at ten to complete your offboarding. For that one, you may want to wear a pair of pants.

HUSBAND: (*beat, a moment for this to sink in*) Never.

HR BRIANNA: Really sticking to the 'no pants' thing–

HUSBAND: Yeah!!! Well! Well, as– as one *gigantic* piece of *shit* once told me, "People change!" And I *just* did. Yeah. And I change my mind; I'd actually rather have my dignity than– than… "lots" of money, so screw you! (*beat*) You're the one that told me that by the way. Piece of shit! (*beat*) And I bet you're wearing pants right now like a loser. (*HR Brianna stands, pants-less… beat*) Okay? I don't even care about that at all.

HR BRIANNA: You just monologued about pants for, like, three minutes. I think you *do* care–

HUSBAND: (*fast*) Maybe I do, maybe I don't! Get out of my face!

HR BRIANNA: This is *my* meeting.

HUSBAND: Bye!

HR BRIANNA: (*beat, nothing changes*) Are you–

HUSBAND: Bye!!!

HR BRIANNA: Goodbye.

HUSBAND: BYE– okay…

*Beat. Nothing changes. HR Brianna can't figure out how to remove him from the room.*

HR BRIANNA: Mr. Dickwad?

HUSBAND: (*furious, ala Dennis Reynolds*) Yeah?!

HR BRIANNA: (*beat*) How do I–

HUSBAND: (*rapid with frustration*) "Participants," hover on "Dickwad," "More," "Remove."

HR BRIANNA: (*beat*) Thank you, Mr. Dickwad.

SFX: LOG OFF

*HR Brianna kicks Husband from the call. He turns on the First Movement of Beethoven's* Moonlight Sonata.

SFX: MOONLIGHT SONATA M.1

*He grabs a remarkably convenient cardboard box and packs up his desk. He sits for a moment before:*

HUSBAND: This is *her* fault.

*Husband glares in Professor's direction. A spotlight slowly rises on her as lights fade from Husband's room.*

LIGHTS DOWN

# ACT I, SCENE 4

## THE BREAKOUT TIMEOUT

LIGHTS UP

*There is a general commotion in the classroom, offered in chaotic vignettes. Silently, Kyle is staring off, distraught over Mallory's disappearance. Zack is sleeping in the back. Brianna has yet to show up to class.*

VIOLA: Literally just look up sparticles and you'll see superpartners!

GREGORY: No, you'll discover the article on which my information is based.

PROFESSOR: Guys–

VIOLA: Have you ever even *seen* a science textbook?

GREGORY: Actually, I have. But that matters not, because Facebüch is all your science books combined!

PROFESSOR: None of this is related to the lecture!

GREGORY: (*overlapping*) False.

VIOLA: (*overlapping*) Support your claim!

PROFESSOR: (*beat*) They're… I don't know, they're just opinions!

GREGORY: Opinions? They are *facts*. Are you saying that Covid isn't real?

VIOLA: Yeah! Are you saying that Covid isn't real?

PROFESSOR: No, I am in *no* way saying that! I'm staying inside, wearing a mask– Covid is real, I just don't know if all your "facts" are.

GREGORY: (*beat*) You're saying *sparticles aren't real?*

VIOLA: They *are* real, they just aren't what you're making up!

GREGORY: I'm not making anything up!!!

PROFESSOR: Why are we still talking about this?

VIOLA and GREGORY: Because *I'm* right!!!

PROFESSOR: It doesn't matter who's right. This isn't what we're learning about.

VIOLA: It does matter! Are you saying facts don't matter?

GREGORY: Yeah! Are you saying facts don't matter?

PROFESSOR: I never said that—

GREGORY: You may not have stated it *directly*, but it was certainly implied.

VIOLA: Inferred, at *least*.

PROFESSOR: Wait. Viola, you're right. You *inferred* that I was saying facts don't matter, but your inference wasn't correct. I never *implied*— (*beat*) Okay. All I'm trying to say is I'd *love* if I could get started with my lesson.

VIOLA: You're going to start your lesson without two students in the classroom?

GREGORY: Pfft. Negligent.

*Professor scrambles to get them back to the main room.*

PROFESSOR: Shit– *shoot!* (*beat, gives up on attempting clean language*) Eh, fuck it. Do you know how to get them out? They've been in there for, like, ten minutes–

KYLE: (*staring into space*) Forty minutes.

PROFESSOR: It has *not* been forty minutes. How do–

KYLE: (*seething*) NO! ... No. Two days, three hours, and *forty* minutes since we've touched.

## LIGHTS CROSSFADE STARTS

*Lights slowly crossfade between the main room and the breakout room timeout. Gilbert and Mallory are in the separate call, alone. Kyle and Mallory happen to be saying the same thing, and Professor and Gilbert are as well.*

KYLE and MALLORY: Physical touch is our love language, remember?

PROFESSOR and GILBERT: How could I forget.

## LIGHTS CROSSFADE END

*The crossfade is complete. Full segue into the breakout room, with a brief rewind in time. Conversation continues...*

MALLORY: Well, *clearly* you have! You have made *no* effort to fix this situation.

GILBERT: Literally *what* is there to do?

MALLORY: I don't know, figure it out!

GILBERT: (*sarcastically*) Yes madame! What shall I do?

MALLORY: (*beat*) Show some initiative, I guess.

GILBERT: With what! We're in timeout! As adults! (*beat, realization*) We're in *adult timeout!*

MALLORY: (*whiny*) I wanna be back with Ky-yule!

GILBERT: (*mocking*) I'm right here– *Damnit!!!* Too many damn Kyles.

MALLORY: But your name is Gilbert.

GILBERT: (*sadly*) That's my *last* name. My first name–

MALLORY: (*gasp!*) Kyle?

*Mallory raises a malformed Kyle salute: an ASL "V." It is almost 'asked' like a question.*

GILBERT: Yeah, it–

*Realizing that Gilbert is actually a 'Kyle,' Mallory can't help but swoon over him.*

MALLORY: Oh, Kyle!

GILBERT: (*confused*) What is happening–

MALLORY: Kyle, I can't believe we're touching again!

*Mallory begins lovingly caressing her computer screen.*

GILBERT: No! I'm not–

MALLORY: But you're Kyle!

GILBERT: Yes, but–

MALLORY: Oh!

GILBERT: Oh?

MALLORY: (*simultaneous, swooning*) Oh!

GILBERT: (*simultaneous, disgusted*) Oh?

MALLORY: Kyle, we're so close! *Metaphorically!*

GILBERT: *Stop*!!! Listen. First of all, I am not the right Kyle– not *your* Kyle. My name was Kyle, but it's Gilbert now. And... (*beat, prepares*) I'm gonna say something, and that's because I'm opening up to you. I'm being vulnerable. So just listen and appreciate the fact that I am comfortable enough to do this because this is *really* hard for me. (*beat, a breath*) I may seem like I hate being renamed Gilbert, but that's only because I'm an excellent actor. It was a ruse. I actually... I– I kinda like it... There are so many Kyles in the world–

MALLORY: Oh, *Kyle*–

GILBERT: Hey! Zip it! (*beat, a breath again*) There are so many Kyles in the world that most of the time I feel like a number. Like, "Great! Kyle number four-hundred thousand has thoughts and feelings! Who gives a shit?" (*beat*) But Gilbert? People *care* about Gilbert. Gilbert is *interesting*. Loved. *Praised*, even–

MALLORY: When were you praised?

GILBERT: Okay, what did I *just* say?

MALLORY: And also, like, you *just* realized that you can, like, be whoever you wanna be?

GILBERT: No! What? I– (*beat*) Zip it! I– Look, I *like* the person I've become. I'm leaving the past behind me. I'm leaving Kyle– (*she goes to interrupt*) Don't! (*beat*) I'm leaving *him* behind and transforming, much like a butterfly, into a brand-new Gilbert... I once was a caterpillar, but this class is my chrysalis! And when I emerge, I will emerge more *beautiful* than ever. Triumphantly! Proud and effervescent–

MALLORY: (*epiphany*) I don't have to be with a man!

GILBERT: What? I– How did you get that from my monologue?

MALLORY: I don't *have* to be with a man! To be happy, I don't *have* to be with Kyle!

GILBERT: I'm still confused. I was talking about *my* transformation?

MALLORY: The whole "leaving him behind and transforming" part?

GILBERT: (*beat*) Oh. Yeah, that makes sense.

MALLORY: All this time I've been basing *my life* around men. Around Kyles! When it should've been about me and my *own* happiness!

GILBERT: You're absolutely right.

MALLORY: All this time I've been so *dependent!*

GILBERT: For *sure*–

MALLORY: I've been *blind!* I let loving Kyle rule my life! (*beat*)Did I *ever* love him? Or did I just love the *idea* of him– holy *shit* it all makes sense.

GILBERT: Complete sense!

MALLORY: But I need support if I'm gonna go through with this... Gilbert? Are you with me?!

GILBERT: Yes! I. Am. A. Feminist!

MALLORY: Good. Then here's the plan–

GILBERT: *Love* me a good plan.

MALLORY: When we go back, I'm going to raise my hand and calmly and professionally say, "Professor, I have an announcement."

GILBERT: Good start–

MALLORY: She'll say, "Mallory, that was very calm and professional. By all means, take it away."

GILBERT: Take it away!

MALLORY: Then I'll dump him in front of the whole class!

GILBERT: *Dump his ass!!!* (*holy shit*) Oh. (*stressed*) oh…

MALLORY: That way, I make a statement that says: (*beat, dramatic*) "Mallory is *free!*" (*normal*) And if he says, (*dramatic*) "Why, Mallory? Why would you do this to me? You shattered my heart! I can't believe I'm losing the best I ever had! Why?! Why?! Why?!" (*normal*) I'll say, "Gilbert persuaded me. He opened my eyes!"

GILBERT: (*scared*) I really don't think that–

MALLORY: Aren't you a feminist?

GILBERT: Yes?

MALLORY: Then why're you silencing female v[*oices*]–

GILBERT: I'm not!!! I– I– (*beat*) Sorry, I definitely silenced you there. Continue.

MALLORY: Yeah. You did. (*clears throat*) Then *why* are you silencing female voices?

GILBERT: I would never do that! I just think you shouldn't go through with this!

MALLORY: I *have* to! I started my transformation and I can't stop now! I'm like a— *(furiously thinking)* I'm like— I'm like a *dam!* I'm like a *burst* dam and I can't stop the flow!

GILBERT: Horrible analogy! Build another dam—

SFX: LOG OFF

BLACKOUT

# ACT I, SCENE 5

## BREAKOUT BREAKUP

LIGHTS UP

SFX: LOG ON

*Professor brings Gilbert and Mallory back from the breakout room. Mallory is about to burst with excitement.*

PROFESSOR: Hey there! Welcome back! *So* sorry for the delay. We were just having a thorough discussion about… (*sigh*) sparticles.

KYLE: Mallory, I've never been so happy to [*see you*]—

MALLORY: (*bloodcurdling scream*) KYLE, I'M BREAKING UP WITH YOU!

*The entire class is stunned, and there is a moment of prolonged silence. Kyle is confused, Gilbert is trying to hide himself, and Mallory is simply overjoyed.*

MALLORY: (*chilling crazy person laughter*) Ha! Ha-haHa-HAHAHAHAHAHA!!! I'm free! I'm free!!!

KYLE: (*ultra serious*) Which one?

MALLORY: There is only *one* Kyle now.

*Mallory acknowledges Gilbert's transformative journey as he sinks further into his seat.*

KYLE: (*deadly serious*) Well? Which one?

MALLORY: Don't act like you—

KYLE: (*ultra very super deadly serious*) Which. One.

MALLORY: (*beat*) You. I'm leaving you behind.

*Kyle stares out into space, unable to process the information.*

*The class is still in shock. There is another prolonged beat.*

SFX: CHAT NOTIFICATIONS

ZACK: (*in chat*) damn.
>wanna go out

MALLORY: No, Zack. I'm going on a transformative journey.

SFX: CHAT NOTIFICATION

ZACK: (*in chat*) ill come with

MALLORY: I'm going alone. Open road, just me and my journey.

VIOLA: I've had a few of those. They're nice.

GREGORY: Very transformative.

*Viola and Gregory air high-five. Another prolonged beat. No one really knows what to do. Kyle is processing, staring out into nothingness. The class watches him for a moment, looking for a reaction. Professor tries to jump in—*

PROFESSOR: I'm honestly not sure how to move on. Uh. My condolences? To both of you?

*Kyle takes a prolonged breath and revs up to grieve.*

PROFESSOR: (*clocking this*) Okay, here we go.

KYLE: (*exact same as before*) Mallory!!! No! Noooo-hoo-hoooo-hoooooo!!! (*collapsing to his knees, weeping*) Forty-*one* minutes… And now, *forever…*

PROFESSOR: (*beat*) Kyle, I am so sorry. You— you can be dismissed for the day if you'd like. I won't hold it against you.

48

KYLE: No! No… I want to stay. I want… to *stay*. I need to be strong. Like *Kyle*…

*Everyone's attention swivels to Gilbert. He hides.*

VIOLA: Gilbert?

KYLE: (*sob*) No, he's a puny bitch.

GILBERT: (*under his breath*) What the fuck?

VIOLA: Your dad, or something?

KYLE: No! (*sob*) Kyle Prime. (*sob*) He's the leader of the Kyle Club.

*Kyle raises a once-freakin' dope-ass salute in the form of the ASL "K," now ripe with floppy sadness.*

GILBERT: There's a *club*?!

GREGORY: Correction. *Cult.*

MALLORY: You don't wanna be a part of that, Gilby.

GILBERT: But why wasn't I invited *originally*?

KYLE: (*ugly sobs*) YOU AREN'T COOL ENOUGH–

PROFESSOR: Okay! Okay. I think we all just need a little break. Let's just take a breather. We (*sigh*) haven't started the lecture yet, but let's take five. We'll get started with 'A Temporary Matter' when we [*get back*]–

LIGHTS DOWN

*All of the videos instantly go off. Professor's tile is isolated in spotlight. All others mute and do their own thing. Kyle curls into a ball, weeping. Gregory sprays his room with Lysol, etc. There is a beat of empty silence where Professor is just… alone.*

49

PROFESSOR: (*sigh, extremely disappointed*) Okay.

*She downs a gulp of wine and crosses to Husband's room.*

LIGHTS FADE

# ACT I, SCENE 6

## THE HAPPY COUPLE

LIGHTS UP

SFX: MOONLIGHT SONATA M.1

*Lights crossfade from the main room to the bedroom, where Husband has been listening to the first movement of* Moonlight Sonata *on repeat and* really *feeling it. He is applying stark white stage makeup, ala Diana Damrau's 'Queen of the Night.' A box of his packed office supplies sits on his desk. Professor enters the room.*

PROFESSOR: (*sadly*) Hi.

*This startles Husband. He runs to turn off his music and spins back to face her. His makeup gleams.*

HUSBAND: (*beat, secretively*) Hi.

*Beat. Professor stares at Husband, who stares back from behind pure white grease paint. She is beyond confused.*

PROFESSOR: I don't wanna know. (*moves on*) How was your meeting?

HUSBAND: (*lying*) Oh– oh, great! Everything went great. *Wonderful.* Got that promotion just like I thought! Making more money now. Like… lots. So, I decided to celebrate.

*Husband gestures to his stage makeup, which is apparently his 'celebration.' Professor is immediately jealous.*

PROFESSOR: Celebrate. That's nice–

HUSBAND: Yeah, so I packed up my things 'cause I figured that managers need new manager stuff.

PROFESSOR: Sure?

HUSBAND: (*rummaging*) Like manager Post-its. Ya know, with little... fuckin... whatever. Uh, manager pens, for... writing. Well, and obviously, manager... (*beat*) Rubik's Cube.

PROFESSOR: For...?

HUSBAND: (*beat*) Cubing.

PROFESSOR: (*jealous*) That's— that's great. About the promotion. I'm confused about the manager stuff though, you can't use [*what you had?*]—

HUSBAND: (*simmering with hidden anger*) Oh, well if it doesn't make sense to you then it's def'nit'ly not *correct* so I should prob'ly just— (*dumps the box out onto the floor*) There.

PROFESSOR: (*A beat of awkward silence as she waits for Husband to ask about her meeting, then...*) Okay. (*another beat*) Are you gonna clean that up?

HUSBAND: Yeah, probably later.

PROFESSOR: Okay. (*beat*) Are you planning on asking me about *my* meeting?

HUSBAND: (*dryly*) Yes— how was your meeting?

PROFESSOR: It was— (*beat, she debates honesty... she lies*) It was great. We're taking a break because the conversation was just so... great. Stimulating, really. Everyone is really engaged, and kind, and... they just really *want* to learn. Which is what every teacher wants—

HUSBAND: Wow that's good, that's good. So, I have to get back to my meeting. Manager stuff now. Manager calculator! … Math.

PROFESSOR: (*beat*) Yeah, I should head back too.

*Another awkward pause. Husband takes a seat on the floor, collecting his things. He doesn't say a word.*

PROFESSOR: Okay. Bye.

*He doesn't return the goodbye. She clocks this and exits. Husband stands to watch her leave, up to something...*

LIGHTS FADE

## ACT I, SCENE 7
## THE DISRUPTION

LIGHTS UP

*Professor returns to the main room, where only her tile is lit. She takes her seat.*

PROFESSOR: Alright, let's get back to it. Cameras on guys. (*nothing changes*) C'mon, cameras please.

SFX: CHAT NOTIFICATION

GILBERT: (*in chat*) not five minutes yet

PROFESSOR: (*building with intensity*) I don't care. We're starting. We are *actually* starting now. No more interruptions, no more sparticles, no— no name calling, no speaking out of turn, no PDA, no pants, no breakups! We are *starting* the lecture. We are actually, *finally* starting. (*the class turns their cameras on one by one*) Thank you. Everyone open your copy of 'A Temporary Matter.' (*they do*) Okay. 'A Temporary Matter' is a short story—

SFX: QUEEN OF THE NIGHT

*Husband dramatically bursts into the main room, sporting full Diana Damrau 'Queen of the Night' makeup and costume. Her aria from* The Magic Flute *blasts over a Bluetooth speaker.*

HUSBAND: (*bloodcurdling*) Wear my *stupid* costume?! Cover my tiny white legs?! Okay *DEAR*!!!

*Husband 'sings' and 'dances' along with the Queen of the Night. Professor frantically tries to turn off her camera.*

PROFESSOR: What? Stop! Stop–

HUSBAND: No! (*singing with the aria*) HA-A-A-A-HA-HA-HA-HA-HA-HA-HA-HAAAAAAA!!!

PROFESSOR: (*frantically*) I'm so sorry, give me one second– just– just don't look! DON'T LOOK AT HIM!!! How do I turn this off?

SFX: LOG ON

*Bri finally logs in. She is intensely confused, then amused.*

BRI: Here professor– *woah*…

HUSBAND: You… CA-A-A-A-HA-HA-HA-HA-HA-HA-HA-HA-HAAAAAAAAAAANNTT!!!

PROFESSOR: Why?!

HUSBAND: I-IT-I-IS-BE-CAUSE-YOU-SUCK-AT-TECH-NO-LO-GYYYYYYYYYYYYYY!!!

PROFESSOR: I do not! I– I'm gonNA *KILL YOU!!!*

*Professor can't figure out how to turn off her camera, so she turns to Husband and chases him like a football player.*

HUSBAND: (*squeal*) AAHHHH! GET AWAYYY!!!

PROFESSOR: GET! OVER! HERE!

*Pure chaos: Professor and Husband ad-lib it up during the chase while Gilbert, Gregory, and Mallory ad-lib according to their prompts. Viola and Bri may ad-lib as well, not as loud as the others. Kyle stares off into space. Zack sleeps.*

GILBERT: Fight! Fight! Fight! (*etc.*)

GREGORY: Social Distancing! Sparticles! (*etc.*)

MALLORY: Follow your heart! Take your *journey*! (*etc.*)

*Husband is flanked to the bedroom, where he leaps onto the bed and tosses possessions from his box at Professor to defend himself. She grabs a nearby book to use as a shield.*

HUSBAND: (*as an item is thrown*) Stop!

PROFESSOR: (*as she dodges/blocks*) No!

HUSBAND: (*throws something else*) Stay back!

PROFESSOR: (*dodges/blocks*) No!

HUSBAND: (*throws something else*) Fire!

PROFESSOR: (*dodges/blocks*) Stop!

HUSBAND: (*throws something else*) No!!!

PROFESSOR: (*dodges/blocks*) Yes!!!

HUSBAND: *BARRAGE!*

*Husband throws the rest of the items in one giant toss, as if he was hurling a bucket of water. He uses the distraction to sprint past her into the front rooms. She chases, and they run two laps (more if it's funnier) around the stage before Professor corners him in the bedroom and slams the door behind them. The ad-libs end and the students eavesdrop, whispering. The following are simultaneous conversations. The left column should flow naturally, and the right column should be said as it falls in conjunction with the left column.*

*P: Professor, H: Husband, GR: Gregory, V: Viola, GI: Gilbert, B: Bri, M: Mallory, K: Kyle, Z: Zack.*

| | |
|---|---|
| P: What is *wrong* with you?! | |
| H: I was just— | GR: What are they saying? |
| P: Just— just what? *Ruining* my class? Just when I'm *finally* about to start after | V: We shouldn't be listening! |
| | GI: SHH! I can't tell, Greg. |

56

dealing with forty minutes of bullshit, you burst in wearing that fucking costume? Seriously, what in your brain made you—

H: (*realizes her lie*) What? I though the conversation was just so… *great*. I thought everyone was *sooo* attentive.

P: I lied! It's been a *horrible* day, no thanks to you, my husband, who is supposed to support me—

H: Support you? What do you *think* I've been doing the last two years? Here I am, invisible again! You can't even *see* me! It's *you* who hasn't been there for *me*!

P: Explain how you've ever been there for me!

H: Huh. Let's just look at today, shall we? I set up your meeting, I checked on you, I was your personal fucking servant—

P: Oh, *please*—

H: —not to mention that all I do is work. For *you*. For us. But you can't see that.

P: By "work," do you mean throwing on a dress, some pretty makeup, and dancing around to sabotage my class?

GR: Don't call me that, *Kyle*.

GI: Don't call me Kyle, *Greg*.

B: What's happening?

M: Oooooh, she lied!

V: No, she didn't!

M: Called it.

B: I'm so fucking confused

GI: Marital crisis.

B: Ah.

GI: Wanna place bets on—

GR: Shhhhh!

B: He did look hot as hell in that dress.

H: That's what *you* told me to do! I was only doing what *you* said when *you* freaked out on me! I just thought it might cheer you up! I don't know—

P: Are you actually *insane*? I was mad! I'm sorry that you pissed me off and I said something ironic, and you took it seriously.

H: Okay, that was *not* an apology.

P: You're right. It wasn't. I shouldn't be apologizing to you. *You* should be apologizing to *me*.

H: What? Are you serious?

P: Absolutely.

H: (*long beat*) No.

P: No?

H: No.

V: I saw his undies.

B: The *one* day I miss class—

ALL: Shhhhhh!

K: I feel that bro.

M: What?

Z: (*unmuted during Husband's beat*) This shit's juicy A.F.

---

*Professor storms out of the room and slams the door behind her again. She is furious but clocks the meeting still running on her computer. She takes a moment to angrily shake off her nerves and then returns to the call. The students pretend they haven't been eavesdropping.*

PROFESSOR: (*sweet and fake*) Hey there, sorry about that! (*silence*) Wow. Quiet. (*joking*) First time that's happened this whole lesson! (*silence*) Right? (*beat*) Uh, okay. I guess we can— *finally* start. 'A Temporary Matter' is—

VIOLA: I think you *do* owe him an apology.

58

PROFESSOR: (*beat*) What?

VIOLA: Not to say he shouldn't also apologize to you.

KYLE: Love is being willing to be wrong and apologizing first.

PROFESSOR: What? Were you eavesdropping–

GILBERT: Not on purpose. You were loud as hell.

PROFESSOR: So, you only pay attention when I'm having marital problems?

VIOLA: Isn't that what the story is about?

MALLORY: I was taking notes.

PROFESSOR: Notes? Notes! *Mallory* was taking *notes*!

MALLORY: Yeah, for what my life would've looked like without a transformative journey. I was thinking about writing an essay–

PROFESSOR: Usually you pay attention in class first.

BRI: (*teacher's pet*) I was! I was paying attention! And I've been here the *whole* time.

ZACK: Me too. So attentive and… *here*.

PROFESSOR: Wow! And now Zack contributes in a *normal* tone for the first time this whole class. What's gotten into you all? People taking notes and not screaming at each other about sparticles– this is a *revelation*! And you know, (*sarcasm*) I am so proud of you all–

KYLE: Thank you!

PROFESSOR: And Kyle! You're the *only* person in this class whose horrible behavior I can actually forgive. After all, you were dumped in front of the entire class.

KYLE: Yeah, I'm still not comfortable talking about it. Like when a relationship ends, you go through the process of grieving? I'm still at 'Shock,' and sort of teetering on the edge of 'Denial.' But regardless, I'm on your husband's side.

PROFESSOR: You're– (*scoffs*) Well I bet Mallory is on *my* side.

MALLORY: (*beat*) I'm on my *own* side, I think.

PROFESSOR: That's– ya know what? That's fine. It's fine! I don't *need* you. I don't need any of you, and I don't need to put up with this bullshit, and you don't get to talk about my life like you know anything about me. Because you don't. We've known each other for what, forty minutes? And for each and every one of those forty minutes you've done nothing but be disruptive and disrespectful. And you know what? I'm on the side of just forgetting all of that and moving on, as long as I get to start my lesson. I will move past everything that's happened if I can just *start* teaching– that's all I want. But you *do* have to be present, and *listen* to what I say, and *do* the work. You don't get to act out, to scream and fight about nonsense, to interrupt me again and again, to talk back to me, or to make this class about yourself, because it's not about you. (*beat*) Can we start now?

*No response. Professor finally has control of her classroom. She knows that her next words will not be interrupted.*

PROFESSOR: Great. So... in 'A Temporary Matter' by Jhumpa Lahiri, we focus on a couple who try to mend their strained marriage by sharing secrets during nightly power outages—

SFX: LOG OFF

PARTIAL BLACKOUT

*A single spotlight falls on Professor. The power goes out, and the call goes down. She collapses her head in her hands.*

TOTAL BLACKOUT

# INTERMISSION: 10 MINUTES

## SFX: BRAHMS OP. 80

Brahms: Academic Festival Overture, op. 80 *plays as a projection of "**INTERMISSION**" or a timer counting down replaces the classroom on the projector screen. Brahms' overture plays throughout the entirety of intermission, and the break should be timed to coincide with the 10-minute piece.*

*Professor spends intermission onstage, failing to fix the power. She searches on her phone, paces around the space, and continually attempts to turn her computer on. She can absolutely take breaks or spend intermission offstage. It is also possible for Husband to be in his room as well. Above all, though, prioritize health. If the actors need a break, take a break!*

*Staging for intermission could be timed with the music to create absurdly dramatized comedy. It should not be dance though.*

# ACT II, SCENE 1

## SEPARATED CHAOS

*Professor is meandering, still attempting to fix the power. Spotlight on Husband, now on a phone call. He is still in full Queen of the Night makeup and costume.*

HUSBAND: (*a bit frantic*) So, it's all dark now, and– and all this started because she wouldn't let me not wear pants. I'm just– I– (*beat*) I've spent so long supporting her that that's all she sees me as. Like a side character in the story of *her* life. Like I don't have my *own* wants and needs. Like I can just be *controlled.*

SFX: EMAIL RECEIVED

*Spotlight on HR Brianna, on the other end of the call.*

HR BRIANNA: One question, Mr. Dickwad. I'm just a tad confused–

HUSBAND: For the *last* time. My name isn't Dickwad.

HR BRIANNA: Oh, right. Sorry about that. It's just, I don't know your real name because I don't care to learn it.

HUSBAND: (*beat*) So, did you have a question? Or–

HR BRIANNA: Ah! Yes– yes. (*breath, then*) Why are you still talking to me? I just fired you.

HUSBAND: (*beat*) Well, I can't talk to her, can I? At least it *feels* like I can't.

HR BRIANNA: Why don't you call a friend?

HUSBAND: (*beat*) You're my only friend.

HR BRIANNA: A-ha. How depressing.

SFX: EMAIL RECEIVED

*Husband and HR Brianna go dark. Spotlight on Gilbert shouting to his* MOM *while playing video games.*

GILBERT: (*to the wings*) Yeah! And then her meeting crashed! Like, can she not work a computer?!

MOM: (*laughing, then yelling from offstage*) Yeah Kyle! She prob'ly shouldn't be a professor then!

GILBERT: Wait! Wait! Wait! (*beat*) Mom?!

MOM: Yeah son?

GILBERT: Call me *Gilbert* now!

MOM: *WHAT?!*

GILBERT: Call me Gilbert! I'm changing my name to Gilbert!

MOM: So your name is gonna be Gilbert *Gilbert*?!

GILBERT: (*beat*) I– I didn't really think about that!

SFX: EMAIL RECEIVED

*Gilbert goes dark. Spotlight on Gregory, who is thoroughly Lysol-ing his room. He sprays Lysol everywhere. Maybe even into his hands to rub into his face and arms like sunscreen. This scene lasts, like, six seconds.*

SFX: EMAIL RECEIVED

*Gregory goes dark. Spotlight on Mallory, who is alone in her room, mumble-singing while her fake nails furiously tap her phone. Kyle sneaks up to her room by pantomime climbing through the window. He creeps in behind her.*

MALLORY: (*mumble-singing*) Goin' on a journey: me, myself, and I. Somethin' somethin' somethin' spread my wings and fly. (*rockstar mode*) I don't need any Kyle to [*tell me how to live!*]–

KYLE: (*sped through*) Why'd you break up with me?!

MALLORY: DAAAAAAHHHH! (*beat*) Jesus!

KYLE: Why, Mallory? Why would you do this to me? You shattered my heart! I can't believe I'm losing the best I ever had! Why?! Why?! Why?!

MALLORY: Gilbert persuaded me. He opened my eyes.

KYLE: Gilbert? (*beat*) *Gilbert?!*

SFX: EMAIL RECEIVED

*Mallory and Kyle go dark. Spotlight on Gilbert.*

GILBERT: (*still shouting*) You don't have to *understand*, Mom! I just want to be *respected*!

MOM: IT SAYS KYLE ON YOUR BIRTH CERTIFICATE!

SFX: EMAIL RECEIVED

*Gilbert goes dark. Spotlight on Zack, who immediately changes character from Mom to regular Zack.*

ZACK: (*snoring*) hhnnnnggghhhh…gahwk-gahwk… hhhnnnnnnugh… grrr…grr…

SFX: EMAIL RECEIVED

*Zack goes dark. Spotlight on Viola. She is studying the textbook, violently flipping pages and scribbling notes.*

VIOLA: *(fast, frantic, and furious)* It seems as though our professor can't function with technology, or… teach. Like *every* other professor. I suppose I'll just have to teach myself! *Again!* *(beat)* Maybe they should be required to get a *degree* in *teaching* to *teach!* *(sigh, reading)* 'A Temporary Matter is'–

SFX: EMAIL RECEIVED

*Viola goes dark. Spotlight on Professor. She calls Husband's former company to help fix her situation.*

PROFESSOR: Yes. *(beat)* Yes, and then everything went dark. *(beat)* No, I didn't trip the breaker, that only happens when, like, four microwaves are plugged in– I was just sitting at my desk, teaching my class– *(beat)* I was on a video call. *(beat)* Yes, I'm wearing pants! *(to herself)* What-the-fuck? *(beat)* I'm sorry. *(beat)* Please. *(beat)* Yes, as soon as you're available.

SFX: EMAIL RECEIVED

*Professor goes dark. Spot on Gregory perusing Facebüch.*

GREGORY: Huh. *(beat)* No, no that cannot be. *(beat)* What the H-E-double-C-K? Dad! Dad?!

DAD: Yes, my child, fruit of my loins?

GREGORY: I was perusing some academic journals–

DAD: On Facebüch?

GREGORY: On Facebüch.

DAD: *Good*, good. You simply don't know who to trust anymore.

GREGORY: (*beat*) Yeah, Dad. Well, I was just doing my daily research, ya know? Sparticles, adjournorites, politigraphs, the norm.

DAD: Politigraphs? That's propaganda from the upper-left-right pinion, son!

GREGORY: I know, I know! But due to its status, being posted on Facebüch and all, it must be *true*, correct?

DAD: Absolutely.

GREGORY: Well anyway, this— this journal arose that basically said Facebüch is full of lies, and I'm just... *confused.*

DAD: Well, that seems like a bit of a paradox. Did it have a special name?

GREGORY: Yeah, sort of. "Facebüch-is-full-of-lies-an-insider-reveals-the-truth."

DAD: That doesn't seem too special to me—

GREGORY: I know, but it's still posted, right? Like it's *posted* posted. On the front page.

DAD: (*mumbling as he scrolls*) No special name... it was posted... I'm... I... I just don't know! Normally I would say this is the truth— it's posted on Facebüch after all! (*beat*) But that would make this also a lie, and then if that's a lie then it can't be the truth— then— what? ... What! ... *What?!*

GREGORY: I know! What do we believe?!

67

SFX: EMAIL RECEIVED

*Gregory goes dark. Spotlight on Gilbert, who is still shouting to his mom, who remains offstage. Kyle sneaks up to Gilbert's room.*

GILBERT: I'll pay to change it myself! I don't want to be Kyle–

KYLE: (*scary*) Hello.

GILBERT: GAHHHHHHH!

KYLE: *Shhhhhhhh*, I just want to talk, Gilby. For now.

MOM: (*yelling from offstage*) Don't *scream* at me, Kyle! I am your *MOTHER!!!*

GILBERT: (*to Mom*) Call me Gilbert– (*to Kyle*) Talk? That's it? Just talking. No hitting?

MOM: I named you! I looked up the most popular baby names and there it was! *Kyle!*

KYLE: If the conversation goes in the right direction.

GILBERT: (*to Mom*) It's so popular that I'm not special! (*to Kyle*) Okay! Okay! What do you wanna know?

MOM: And now, all of a sudden, you just want to switch?! You wanna be *Gilbert?!*

KYLE: Did you or did you not persuade Mallory to dump me?

GILBERT: (*to Mom*) I didn't! *Shit*, no– I– I just had a realization! (*to Kyle*) I didn't at all!

MOM: What?! You didn't *what?!* You had a "realization?" It's called *puberty*, Kyle, it's probably just a phase!

KYLE: Mallory seems to think differently.

GILBERT: (*to Mom*) It's not a phase, Mom!

> *Mom and Gilbert rant at the same time, overlapping. Miraculously, they say "Gilbert Gilbert" at the same time.*

MOM: (*overlapping, muffled mocking*) "It's not a phase Mom! It's not a phase! I'm a grown-up man now and I can make my own decisions! My Mommy still dresses me, but I can change my birth certificate! My name is 'Gilbert Gilbert' now, apparently! I live at home for free and I don't have a job but I'm a big grown-up man!" *Christ!*

GILBERT: (*overlapping, to Kyle*) Okay! Here's how it went. We were stuck in the breakout room, she was going on and on about how she misses you or whatever the shit, I told her about how I wanted to change my name to 'Gilbert Gilbert,' and then, all of a sudden, she stole my transformative journey for herself and decided to dump you! (*beat, no longer overlapping*) There. That's all that happened.

KYLE: (*beat*) Your name is gonna be Gilbert *Gilbert?*

SFX: EMAIL RECEIVED

> *Kyle and Gilbert go dark. Spotlight on Gregory and Dad.*

GREGORY: (*beat, disturbed silence*) So.

DAD: (*beat*) So…

GREGORY: (*beat*) I'm unsure how to proceed in life.

DAD: Ditto.

GREGORY: Do we… delete Facebüch?

DAD: (*beat*) *What?*

GREGORY: Do we purge that which hath stained our life with misinformation?

DAD: (*beat, thinks*) No. We keep it.

GREGORY: But how will we ever be free?

DAD: We use it *against* itself. Fight sparticles with sparticles!

GREGORY: Yeah! (*beat*) Yeah. (*beat*) Dad?

DAD: Yeah, son?

GREGORY: (*beat*) I don't think sparticles are real.

SFX: EMAIL RECEIVED

*Spotlight on Husband, who is no longer on a call. He paces.*

HUSBAND: (*reluctantly putting pants on*) Horrible. I feel horrible– that was a *horrible* idea– (*to himself*) Why did I do that?

BLACKOUT

# ACT II, SCENE 2
## THE IT GUY

DIM LIGHTS UP

*Professor, now masked, opens her door and IT Zachary enters, sporting a fluorescent vest-mask combo. They both hold flashlights. IT Zachary talks with a fluctuating Minnesotan accent (don't drag the pace).*

IT ZACHARY: What type a' outage we got here? Internet? Cable?

PROFESSOR: Electric, I think. The lights are out.

IT ZACHARY: Oh! I thought that was a cultural thing.

PROFESSOR: (*beat*) No, there's a power outage.

IT ZACHARY: Okay? I– don't know why ya called me and not'cher landlord or yer electric company.

PROFESSOR: Oh. Well– I don't know, usually my husband handles this kind of thing, but he's–

IT ZACHARY: Too depressed about losin' his job? I heard. *Really* sucks.

PROFESSOR: What? Losing his job?

IT ZACHARY: Yeah man, it's really rough out here for us white male IT workers. Our firm had to make some crazy cuts, and he just didn't make it. Shame, really. He was one a my favorite people there. My best work friend, really. Speakin' a your husband– uhhhh… (*beat*) whatever his name was– why didn't ya ask him to help?

PROFESSOR: Well, he's–

IT ZACHARY: Too depressed about losin' his job? (*clicks his tongue*) Damn.

PROFESSOR: Yeah. Sure.

IT ZACHARY: Well, I'm happy to help. For a, uh— *price,* a'course.

PROFESSOR: Well yeah, whatever your rate is—

IT ZACHARY: You know— funny thing— this really reminds me of that one scene in *The Drowsy Chaperone.* Ever seen it?

PROFESSOR: No. Is that a movie?

IT ZACHARY: Musical (*jazz hands*).

PROFESSOR: Oh. You're one of *those* people.

IT ZACHARY: Oh, you betcha! I 'specially like *Drowsy* cause it's a musical that makes fun of other musicals. Then in the end— get this— the main guy kills himself.

PROFESSOR: That's… really dark.

IT ZACHARY: Well, that's just my speculation a' course. Ya know, he's drinkin', takin' pills, then he joins the story and flies away in an airplane? Yeah, he's dead for sure.

PROFESSOR: (*beat*) My power?

IT ZACHARY: Oh! Your power! Your power, sorry, totally forgot! (*IT Zachary crosses to the breaker*) Yeah, so the scene I'm talkin' about is basically the same as this, like the landlord comes in, makes some *sexual advances,* checks the breaker, flips this switch here, and (*flips the breaker*) boom!

LIGHTS UP

*The stage is now empty... no students to be seen.*

IT ZACHARY: *(cont.)* Then some music plays, but it's probably copyrighted, so I can't sing it. But it goes a lil' somethin' like "skyyyyyyyy"–

PROFESSOR: What? It was that easy?

IT ZACHARY: Okay, I was singin' and you cut me off.

SFX: COMPUTER STARTUP

*Their attention snaps to her computer as the projector glows to life, presenting its startup screen. After a beat, it fades to Professor's photo album screensaver. Zachary cringes.*

IT ZACHARY: Well, that certainly ruined the moment. But yeah, it appears ya tripped your breaker. Not sure what caused it. Didja, by chance, have four microwaves plugged in?

PROFESSOR: No, I told you that on the phone–

IT ZACHARY: Maybe a vibrator or somethin'?

PROFESSOR: What? No!

IT ZACHARY: Damn. Woulda been useful.

PROFESSOR: *(beat, thinks)* Who the hell has a cord-powered vibrator?

IT' ZACHARY: *(shrugs)* It's more powerful. AAAnyway, let's get to the bottom of this. So... *(he wiggles his eyebrows at her)* what exactly were ya doin' when everythin' went dark?

PROFESSOR: I was teaching.

IT ZACHARY: Online?

PROFESSOR: Yeah?

IT ZACHARY: Oh! (*beat*) Yeah, that don't make sense.

PROFESSOR: No, it doesn't.

IT ZACHARY: Ya know, sometimes it don't have to. Sometimes, ya just feel what'cher feelin', and it don't make sense. Like a... warm fluttery tinglin' in your crotchular region...

PROFESSOR: What the fuck? I'm *married*–

IT ZACHARY: Damnit! *DAMNIT!* Yer right! What's his name. What's his name? Uhh, uh–

*IT Zachary rushes to the desktop to see if he can put a name to Husband's face in the screensaver album.*

IT ZACHARY: M-Matt? *No*... uh, whatever! Yer right; that was unprofessional. I just figured that since that's what happens in *Drowsy*, and the drive was really far, and I used all that expensive gasoline to get here, and I was just thinkin'– like "Oh, she might pay me in a *different* way..."

PROFESSOR: Get the fuck out.

*IT Zachary frantically scrambles to exit the apartment.*

IT ZACHARY: Oh, you betcha! Don't forget to leave a review of yer experience!

*IT Zachary exits, and Professor slams the front door.*

BLACKOUT

# ACT II, SCENE 3
## OFFBOARDING

SFX: LOG ON

LIGHTS UP

*Husband joins HR Brianna on another call. There are several others attending: Executive, Manager, and CIO. None of them have cameras on, just black silhouettes, and their microphone icons carry red strikethroughs.*

*Husband is still wearing makeup. He tries to get comfortable in his pants.*

HR BRIANNA: So, Mr. Dickwad, we are going to perform a brief exit interview to understand your experience at our company. Sound good? (*beat, silence*) Alright. Do you mind if our call is recorded for legal purposes?

*Beat, silence again. She starts recording regardless.*

SFX: RECORDING MEETING

HR BRIANNA: Alright, let's begin. How do you feel about the company's decision to downsize?

HUSBAND: Bad.

HR BRIANNA: Mmm. Tough. (*beat*) Did you feel that the company communicated well about the situation and the changes it was facing?

HUSBAND: No.

HR BRIANNA: Ooh, interesting. Not what I expected! (*beat*) How would you describe your relationship with your supervisor?

HUSBAND: Worse than I thought. You still don't know my name, Brianna.

HR BRIANNA: Indeed. Indeed I do not. (*beat*) Mr. Dickwad, were you able to adapt to remote work?

HUSBAND: (*beat, truthful*) I was. And I used to enjoy it.

HR BRIANNA: Do you think the downsizing was handled with fairness and respect for employees?

HUSBAND: (*beat*) Do you?

HR BRIANNA: I legally cannot say.

HUSBAND: Well. You know *my* answer.

HR BRIANNA: (*beat*) I'll mark that one down as 'N/A.' Is there feedback you'd like to provide about the organization's culture, leadership, policies–

HUSBAND: (*pushing to a different topic*) So this is it?

HR BRIANNA: We cannot legally say, Mr. Dickwad, however–

CIO: (*offstage*) Yeah, this is it.

HUSBAND: (*beat*) Why me?

HR BRIANNA: Sorry?

HUSBAND: Why me? Why is it *me* who you're firing?

HR BRIANNA: Well, to be clear, it's not *just* you.

HUSBAND: But why me and not someone else? It just doesn't seem *fair*–

*HR Brianna pauses the recording.*

SFX: PAUSE RECORDING

HR BRIANNA: (*sigh*) You didn't do anything wrong, Mr. (*doesn't know his name*) … You just– (*beat*) didn't leave an impression. You were fine. Normal. But normal isn't good enough anymore. And you're right. It isn't fair. But business doesn't run on *fair*– sometimes, life is unfair. Do you think it's fair that we have to decide who stays and who goes? Who gets to keep their career for another month before we downsize again? The answer here is that nothing is fair, especially now. (*genuinely trying to help him, still demeaning*) From what we know, the pandemic and its effects will be a temporary matter. With a bit of luck and a better impression, it's possible for you to get your job back. So, give it some time. Maybe you'll get a second look, and maybe *then* you'll earn the respect for us to learn your name.

*HR Brianna resumes the recording.*

SFX: RECORDING MEETING

HR BRIANNA: Sorry for the technical difficulties–

HUSBAND: Do you think it could be you who's to blame?

HR BRIANNA: (*beat*) I'm not sure what you mean.

HUSBAND: I didn't stand out because you never got to know me. How could I stand out to people who don't know I exist?

HR BRIANNA: (*beat*) I legally cannot say.

HUSBAND: (*scoffs*) Right.

HR BRIANNA: Finally, do you feel as though the use of technology to host remote meetings has benefited our company?

HUSBAND: (*beat*) No. I feel like you might've known me if we had actually met.

HR BRIANNA: Great! As of this moment, we have revoked your access to all company systems and disabled your accounts. You will be mailed a box to return your tech. Any missing components will be deducted from your final paycheck, which will be sent upon confirmation of received items. Thank you for working for us.

CIO: (*offstage*) See ya, Matt!

SFX: LOG OFF

*Executive, CIO, and Manager instantly log off. Husband sinks into his chair and closes his laptop.*

SFX: LOG OFF

BLACKOUT

# ACT II, SCENE 4

## ATTENDANCE (AGAIN)

*Professor counts the participants on her screen as the students carry on with ad-libs. Kyle is still at Gilbert's house. The chatter amongst the class ends on:*

PROFESSOR: Okay, is everyone back?

VIOLA: Why don't you take attendance again?

PROFESSOR: You know what? Fine. Attendance. Again. Kyle?

KYLE: (*takes a moment to get 'cool'*)… Aloha.

*Kyle raises the dope-ass ASL 'K' salute.*

PROFESSOR: Gil[*bert*]– Kyle? Why are you at Gilbert's house?

KYLE: Oh. Yeah. I came over to hit him a bunch, but we made up! Turns out I was being irrational, and I need to accept that these events were out of my control–

PROFESSOR: Shut up. Go back home, there's a pandemic. (*back to attendance*) Gilbert.

*Kyle gives Gilbert a deep hug and then leaves his space with a knowing wave. He takes a few laps around the stage during the dialogue below and lands in his tile.*

GILBERT: Here. And thanks for calling me Gilbert–

PROFESSOR: (*moving on*) Yeah, yeah– Viola.

VIOLA: Present. Professor, I have a question–

PROFESSOR: Nope! Gregory.

GREGORY: Currently in attendance.

PROFESSOR: Cool–

GREGORY: Announcement!

PROFESSOR: *Oh my god*–

GREGORY: I would like to take this moment to publicly apologize for my outbursts–

PROFESSOR: (*moving on*) Apology accepted–

GREGORY: I have since concluded that sparticles *aren't* real, and Facebüch *does* contain lies–

PROFESSOR: (*still trying to move on*) That's *great*–

VIOLA: Except they *are* real–

PROFESSOR: Moving on! Zack. (*no response*) Zack?!

ZACK: Yo! Quit making me talk and turn on my microphone and stuff!

PROFESSOR: (*beat*) You can just say "here." Bri. (*no response*) Bri?

BRI: Sorry! I'm here! And I've also been here the whole time, F.I.Y. just for the record.

*Husband enters, nervous and looking guilty.*

PROFESSOR: Great. Mallory?

MALLORY: Here, but not, cause I'm on my journey–

PROFESSOR: Wonderful. 'A Temporary Matter' is–

HUSBAND: Hey, can we talk?

PROFESSOR: What? I'm in the middle of–

HUSBAND: I know! It's just– this is really important.

PROFESSOR: I've been trying to start my class for over an hour now.

HUSBAND: I know, and part of that is my fault–

PROFESSOR: I'm completely aware of that, Mr. I-finally-put-on-some-fucking-pants.

HUSBAND: Well, that's part of it–

PROFESSOR: No, you need to leave and let me start my class.

HUSBAND: But–

PROFESSOR: Leave me alone.

HUSBAND: Hey–

PROFESSOR: *Go!*

*Beat. Husband crosses to the bedroom. He prepares.*

PROFESSOR: So sorry about that; pushing on, 'A Temporary Matter' is–

MALLORY: I feel like you should talk to him.

PROFESSOR: What? *What!?* Please, *please* just let me start my lesson.

KYLE: No, no, listen. When you bottle up your emotions, you explode. Look at Mallory and I–

PROFESSOR: She dumped you because–

VIOLA: I feel like they're right, professor.

GILBERT: Professor, we may have gotten off on the wrong foot. You saw my crotch, you complimented my huge, big manly peepee, you

81

accidentally called me Kyle when my name was
Gilbert– honest mistake– But through this
lecture I feel I've gotten to know you–

PROFESSOR: You couldn't be further from the
truth–

GREGORY: No, we *have* gotten to know you. And
that's *not* propaganda from the upper-left-right
pinion.

MALLORY: And you need to talk to him.

PROFESSOR: I'm in the middle of my lecture–

BRI: You actually didn't *start* yet–

PROFESSOR: I'm aware! I'm *well* aware of that–

KYLE: Avoiding your feelings will only lead to more
pain.

ZACK: Alright, listen up. I fucking *hate* paying
attention, but since you won't shut the fuck up
and let me sleep, it's intervention time, bitch.
You're a needy, overly-anxious woman and
your stress pours over onto him. He pushes
back, you get mad, he pushes back worse– like,
I don't know, sabotaging your career by
bursting into your lecture in full costume
belting *The Magic Flute*. Right? Then, there's the
lying– from *both* of you. You're hiding
something, but he's hiding something too.
Something he's embarrassed of. And lying only
leads to... (*drumroll*) you guessed it! Divorce.
Do you want that? No! Mainly because of the
legal fees. The only obvious answer is to simply
talk to him–

*Husband is barely seen creeping to the breaker panel.*

PROFESSOR: I AM *NOT* TALKING TO HIM!

*Husband flips the breaker.*

BLACKOUT

SFX: LOG OFF (SEVEN TIMES)

# ACT II, SCENE 5

## SOLILOQUY and CONFESSIONS

*Total, utter darkness. The absence of technology seems to break down a barrier of communication. Professor speaks her heart, which is very strained, hurt, and tired.*

PROFESSOR: (*long beat*) Are you serious? Are you actually serious? I am at my fucking wit's end. Is the universe punishing me? Is it impossible to do *anything* today? No! Please! What did I do wrong? Tell me. Explain to me what I did to deserve this– help me understand! (*beat*) Ya know, I probably tripped the breaker. Again. Except, I don't want to even *attempt* to fix it. I don't want to *try*. I want to sit here, in the absence of all this bullshit. Because this is the first moment of peace I've had all day. (*beat*) Do I want to do this every day? Do I deal with this for the rest of my life? What about my other dreams? I paid tens of thousands of dollars to do this, when I could've done anything else? (*beat, to herself*) Oh my god. My *husband* paid for this. He did all that work to get me here. And we can't even *speak* to each other. Why can't we just *talk*?

HUSBAND: (*beat*) I want to talk.

*Professor turns to see Husband behind her in the dark.*

PROFESSOR: (*beat*) I– Me too. I'm– I'm glad you're here... I'm sorry, I don't know what's wrong with me–

HUSBAND: You should *not* be apologizing to me.

PROFESSOR: Yes, I–

HUSBAND: No. I've been horrible, rude, and selfish, and I really don't know why. I've felt distant, but I don't know what in the world made me think ruining your lesson would solve anything, or make me feel better– I... (*beat*) I'm sorry, it's hard– this is hard.

PROFESSOR: No, no; keep going.

HUSBAND: Keep going?

PROFESSOR: Yeah. But start small.

HUSBAND: Okay. I– I've been feeling distant lately–

PROFESSOR: Smaller.

HUSBAND: Oh, okay, uh. I like classical music–

PROFESSOR: No, no. A confession. Something you haven't told me before.

HUSBAND: (*beat*) I... haven't actually been working out. I lost all that weight because– well, I stopped buying McDonalds on the way home from work. Because– well, we're stuck inside.

PROFESSOR: (*long beat*) You know I'm really bad with technology. (*Husband chuckles*) Sometimes, I feel like I could be better, but then I remember that I have you. So, I don't try. And I just rely on you to fix my problems for me.

HUSBAND: I think– I think I was... glorifying the whole pants thing. I think that I was trying to convince myself that this doesn't suck. This all just *really* sucks, and I was trying to find... something... positive.

PROFESSOR: I saw a therapist a while ago. You thought I was at my thesis defense, but I was really there, with her. She said I have anxiety, amidst maybe other... stuff. And I got so scared of facing it that I just couldn't get myself to go back. (*beat*) I never told you. I thought you might see me differently. And she told me she recommends marriage counseling, too, but I didn't want to worry you.

HUSBAND: I lied about the promotion. I *really* thought I was getting one, that I deserved one, but– I lost my job. They had to downsize, and I got cut. She said I was 'fine,' but that I didn't stand out. But the entire time, she couldn't even remember my name. And I realized that I was just a number to them. And numbers aren't special. They *can* be cut, and it doesn't matter. But when did that start applying to people? Real people, not just people you only see through a screen, but real people with real lives and feelings, and... dreams? I just–

PROFESSOR: I know you already know this, but I lied about my lesson being great. It has been... (*a chuckle*) awful. Everyone keeps interrupting me. My students are blatant assholes. There have been *many* thorough discussions about pants and sparticles, someone got dumped in the middle of my class, and I haven't even started the lecture yet. And I just feel... doubt. About *this* being my future. Is this going to be every day? Is *this* what I wanted? (*beat*) You know that feeling when what you *thought* you wanted isn't what it turned out to be? Then, you just feel stupid for *ever* believing otherwise. And so full of regret for not pursuing what you *really* loved. Maybe you convinced yourself you'd end up loving it? Maybe you convinced yourself it was the safe option. Or the *right* option. But now, all you know for certain is that everything you thought you knew was wrong? Where do you go from there?

HUSBAND: It was me. Not just the pants stuff– *wow* I am so… *incredibly* dumb. (*beat*) I flipped the breaker. Both times. I– I don't know, I was really upset. And I've felt like you haven't seen me lately, like I've been in the background of your life. Like I needed some huge intervention to just be *noticed*. And that I was a side character in your story. And I know your lesson was important, but my job is– *was*, really important to me, too. To us. And I have *loved* sitting back and watching you do what you… what you *thought* you wanted to do, even if you're having doubts now. I've loved saying that you're going back to school because of me. That you were settling down, trying to work at a university. And my God, you fucking did it. Like you always do. And I am so proud of you, regardless of if it went great, or if it went like shit. But– I'm just *tired*. I'm tired of feeling like I'm losing myself. (*beat*) Like I'm losing *you*.

PROFESSOR: (*longest beat*) I have one more, but I want to turn the lights on first.

HUSBAND: Okay. (*he crosses to the breaker, bumping into something*) Ow. (*he and Professor share a chuckle*)

## LIGHTS UP

*He flips the breaker. The students are all in their respective tiles, pantomiming a lesson taking place, being led by Viola. Professor and Husband come together in the light.*

PROFESSOR: I'm sorry.

HUSBAND: I am so, *so* sorry. I love you—

## SFX: COMPUTER STARTUP

*Husband is interrupted by Professor's computer booting up. Their attention snaps to computer as the projector glows to life, presenting its startup screen, bathing the theatre in blue. After a beat, it fades to Professor's screensaver: a slideshow of her and Husband's photos. They watch:*

*Their first date, anniversaries, and birthdays.*
*Moving in together.*
*Game nights and parties.*
*Vacations and adventures.*
*Buying a car, a house, or a pet.*
*Husband's proposal…*

*And most importantly, their wedding day.*

*Sometime during the slideshow, Professor and Husband turn away from the computer and notice the projector screen: the first time it's ever been 'visible.' There is a long, beat of reflection.*

PROFESSOR: I love you too.

HUSBAND: (*beat*) I've missed you.

PROFESSOR: I've missed you too.

HUSBAND: (*beat*) We'll be alright– (*beat*) No. Not just alright. We're gonna be great. This is just a– a temporary rough patch. Nothing we can't work through.

PROFESSOR: (*beat, something clicks...*) Huh.

HUSBAND: What?

PROFESSOR: No, uh, it's nothing. Just... really hoping that *all* of this is temporary. (*long beat, they look around*) Maybe it will be. Maybe all of this is just a mistake. One horrible day out of a thousand. Maybe it's not *supposed* to be this way, and we just lost sight of how it *is* supposed to be. (*beat*) Maybe I don't need to start my class to be happy. God knows I'd rather just read a fucking book than lecture about one. If being happy is temporary, maybe the things that make us happy are temporary, too. And we grow. And we change. And life goes where we take it. (*she turns to Husband*) Maybe you don't need your job. (*sudden connection*) Shit! Your job!

HUSBAND: What about it?

PROFESSOR: That Zach guy? Your IT friend?

HUSBAND: Oh! *Zachary? Love* that guy! Well... he's kind of a freak.

PROFESSOR: Yeah. A freaky pervert.

HUSBAND: What?

PROFESSOR: He came over to help me fix the power and he made some… advances.

HUSBAND: (*beat*) Wait, he–

PROFESSOR: If you call them—

HUSBAND: (*a realization*) I could get my job back! They fire him, and I could take his place! Normal is *certainly* better than pervert! I'm— (*realizes his selfishness*) Hold on. Are you okay?

PROFESSOR: (*beat*) Oh, I'm fine! More confused than anything— call them!

HUSBAND: Okay! I call, you start your class.

PROFESSOR: I don't know if I want to.

HUSBAND: You have a couple minutes.

PROFESSOR: So?

HUSBAND: You don't wanna rejoin?

PROFESSOR: (*beat*) Honestly? No. I don't know if it's worth it.

HUSBAND: You've said over and over that all you wanted was to start your lesson. Well… start it.

*Husband bounds to the bedroom. Professor turns and catches another glimpse of her screensaver. She makes a decision.*

*In music terms, Attacca! Immediate segue to the next scene.*

# ACT II, SCENE 6
## VIOLA LEADS THE CLASS

LIGHTS UP

SFX: LOG ON

*Viola picks up the conversation from the pantomime. Zack has his hand raised in a lazy claw.*

VIOLA: Yes, Zack?

ZACK: Is one theme like, outside forces and inside circumstances?

VIOLA: Absolutely! Like the power outages giving the couple opportunities to share secrets.

KYLE: "You have power over your mind– not outside events." Marcus Aurelius. He said that.

VIOLA: Exactly! However, do Shoba and Shukumar prevail, or do they *succumb* to the outside forces?

GREGORY: Well, I think that depends because Shoba sort of sets up the scenario to say she wants to leave him, right? So, she *uses* the outside forces to affect him. Like the government or media does, especially with like, sparticles and stuff.

VIOLA: Well, yes and… well I guess you're right.

MALLORY: Wait… Does Shoba know from the start that they weren't supposed to be together? Because it *certainly* wasn't apparent to me.

KYLE: I– I don't think she did, because if she did, why would she stay with him in the first place, let alone let herself fall in love?

MALLORY: Yeah. I guess you're right. Thanks Kyle.

VIOLA: Speaking of your ex-relationship, another big idea is how easy it is to hurt the ones we love. First, their jabs are unintentional, but as the story goes on, they use the sharing of secrets to almost *purposefully* hurt each other.

PROFESSOR: Like my husband and I today.

VIOLA: Yes! *Just* like that– (*realizes, oh shit!*) Hey! Hey professor, welcome back, we were just–

PROFESSOR: (*slight smile*) Discussing the story.

VIOLA: (*beat*) Well, now that you're back you can take over your lesson if you want to, I guess. So…

PROFESSOR: (*beat*) No, you can keep going. Maybe a student-led thing is what works best for you.

VIOLA: Okay, if that's what *you* want, I'm like totally fine with that, I mean, like, can I use my lesson plans? Well, that's if you want like *one* student to lead and–

PROFESSOR: Sure, Viola. That's fine with me if it's fine with the rest of the class.

GILBERT: Professor?

PROFESSOR: (*beat*) Gilbert?

GILBERT: Sorry.

*Beat. The class gathers the courage to apologize, overlapping one another.*

VIOLA: Sorry Professor.

KYLE: Sorry.

GREGORY: Apologies, m'lady.

MALLORY: I'm sorry.

BRIANNA: Sorry I was late.

SFX: CHAT NOTIFICATION

ZACK: (*a beat later, in chat*) sorry :(

PROFESSOR: (*beat*) It's alright guys. This is… not easy. But I know it can't be easy for you either. And I appreciate you sticking with me today, through everything. (*beat, checks watch*) But it looks like time is just about up for today.

GILBERT: See you on Thursday?

PROFESSOR: (*beat, thinks*) Yeah. Let's try this style again. It seems like it worked better for you. (*beat*) Hey, have a great rest of your day.

STUDENTS: (*ad-lib variations*) "See ya professor," "Goodbye," "See you Thursday," etc.

SFX: LOG OFF (SIX TIMES)

*Spotlights black out on the students in succession. Professor and Viola's squares, and Husband's bedroom, remain lit.*

VIOLA: Professor? (*Professor perks up*) Thank you.

PROFESSOR: Thank *you*, Viola. See you Thursday; don't forget to prepare something.

VIOLA: I'm good for the next month!

*Viola holds up a stack of lesson plans already made before waving and leaving the meeting. Blackout on Viola. Husband re-enters, off the phone.*

SFX: LOG OFF

PROFESSOR: *(to herself)* How in the hell did she write that so fast?

HUSBAND: They fired him.

PROFESSOR: Are you serious–

HUSBAND: Well, they're launching an investigation, and he's suspended in the meantime. Turns out it's happened before, but the company's just kind of swept it under the rug, sooo. Yeah. *(shyly)* But in the meantime, they need someone to replace him…

PROFESSOR: So that means–

HUSBAND: *PROMOTION!*

PROFESSOR: Oh my god! Congratulations–

HUSBAND: *(shyly)* And I turned them down. Boom! They don't need me; I don't need them. I think I do like my dignity more. *(Professor smiles)* Besides, they're probably gonna have to make some *huge* cuts with the lawsuits they're gonna face… Yeah. I'll find a different job that still treats me like shit soon enough. *(they laugh; beat)* How'd your class go?

PROFESSOR: *(beat)* It went… great. For real this time.

HUSBAND: That's awesome.

PROFESSOR: *(beat)* Hey, did you mean what you said?

HUSBAND: Every word. Did you?

PROFESSOR: Yeah.

HUSBAND: *(beat)* I love you.

PROFESSOR: I love you too.

94

FADE TO BLACK

SFX: RUMBLING

*The same rumbling from the beginning...*

*It grows amidst the darkness, while Professor and Husband take their place back in present day. They are transported through the liminal space of technology, through memories, and through time.*

*Therapist enters as the rumbling grows, and grows...*

# ACT II, SCENE 7
## THURSDAY

*The rumbling crescendos, then is abruptly halted by:*

SFX: LOG ON

LIGHTS UP

*Two days later. Professor, Husband, and Therapist are back in their first session of marriage counseling. They sit in silence, awaiting a response from Therapist. He sits in stunned silence, taking it all in.*

THERAPIST: That was *one day?*

HUSBAND: More like an hour and a half.

THERAPIST: *That was an hour and a fucking half???*

PROFESSOR and HUSBAND: Yes.

THERAPIST: *(beat)* I would just like to say that I am *beyond* glad you're here. And I would love to continue the conversation at our next session–

PROFESSOR: Can't we keep going? This was *very* therapeutic.

HUSBAND: I can feel the distance closing already!

*Professor and Husband turn, look at each other in real life across their apartment and share a giggle.*

THERAPIST: Well, you didn't actually *do* anything yet. You rambled on about that *horrible* day for *so long* that we're about half an hour past time. So, no. You can't keep going. What I do suggest, however, is making sure you continue to attend these sessions. You– and I *cannot* express this enough– have *a lot* of work to do. It doesn't just *get better*. If you want this to be a temporary setback, you need to put in the work. Do you understand?

PROFESSOR and HUSBAND: (*beat*) Yes.

THERAPIST: Good. Same time next Thursday?

PROFESSOR: (*overlapping*) Sure.

HUSBAND: (*overlapping*) Sounds great.

THERAPIST: Wonderful. I *will* be billing you for the extra (*checks watch*) thirty-*four* minutes. So, watch out for that.

*Beat. No "goodbye." He sits in awkward silence, before smacking the shit out of his computer:*

SFX: LOG OFF

*The meeting ends, blackout on Therapist's spotlight. What remains is the dim, normal,* real *light of their apartment. There is a moment of silence. Professor and Husband get up from their desks and meet at center. They just look at each other… for a moment, the audience may not know how the show will proceed.*

PROFESSOR: We did it.

HUSBAND: (*beat*) We did it!

PROFESSOR and HUSBAND: *WE DID IT!*

*They celebrate their first step with some adlibs, maybe a high five, and lastly a joyous hug, before:*

HUSBAND: Alright I gotta go!

PROFESSOR: Me too! I'm gonna be late!

*Instant chaos. Instant* fun *chaos. They scatter through the apartment, frantically trying to get ready for their next meetings. It should be reminiscent of their chase earlier, but a joyous, 'we fucking did it' frantic. Ad-lib it up!*

HUSBAND: I love you!

PROFESSOR: Love you too!

*Husband sprints into the bedroom and turns:*

HUSBAND: Hey! Check it!

*He rips his pants off and starts doing that same playful erotic dance or gesture from before.*

PROFESSOR: (*amused*) Stop it!

HUSBAND: Wish me luck!!! *Gotta hype myself up…*

*Husband sprints into the bedroom and slams the door behind him. The* Hallelujah Chorus *blares in the background. He harmonizes screech-ily to hype himself up for an interview.*

### SFX: HALLELUJAH CHORUS

*Professor briefly looks around before ripping her pants off and tossing them to the other room, maybe to an audience member? She sprints over to her desk and rips a sticky note off her computer with technology-help instructions.*

### LIGHTS DOWN

*Spotlight on Professor; the rest of the stage suddenly goes dark, and the* Hallelujah Chorus *fades into the background. The students quickly filter into their spaces and begin pantomiming different conversations.*

*She follows the instructions with precision, logging on to the classroom, this time with no notes, and... no pants!*

SFX: LOG ON

LIGHTS UP

*Lights up on the rest of the class, suddenly having many different ad-libbed conversations while on break. It should sound quite chaotic. Gilbert and Mallory update each other on their journeys, and Kyle is talking at Gregory. Bri has yet to show up, and Zack is trying to sleep. Viola reads the textbook before the log on draws her attention.*

*Optionally, the director may choose to integrate curtain call within this final scene for the 'live in the chaos' theme.*

VIOLA: Ah! *(joking)* Nice to *finally* have you, professor.

PROFESSOR: Sorry I'm late, I—

ZACK: Therapy. We know.

PROFESSOR: How did you—

ZACK: *Nobody else log on so I can fucking sleep, okay?!* *(snoring)* hhnnnnggghhhh...gahwk-gahwk... hhhnnnnnnugh... grrr...grr...

MALLORY: So, my journey is going *great*. What about *your* journey Gilby?

KYLE: Yeah, and then I realized that I don't need a girlfriend to be happy! I'm so *totally* at "acceptance" now! *(ala* Pokémon) *Kyle!*

*Kyle raises the dope-ass ASL "K" for the final time...*

VIOLA: So how was it, professor?

PROFESSOR: We probably shouldn't talk about that—

GILBERT: So… the paperwork to *officially* change my name goes through tomorrow!

GREGORY: Yeah, I'm still at "anger" with my breakup with Facebüch.

PROFESSOR: Hey, Viola, I talked with the university—

VIOLA: And?

MALLORY: That's great! Last step on your *journey*!

KYLE: I'm going on a social media cleanse so I can't relate.

PROFESSOR: … And they can't give you an official position as a TA, or even as a tutor. I'm sorry— something about money?

GILBERT: But my horrible mother wouldn't let me change it—

GREGORY: How will you get your facts and trustworthy news?

VIOLA: No, that's okay! This is too fun to be paid for it anyways!

MALLORY: Oh, she's a *bitch!* It's *your* identity!

KYLE: I suppose I'll have to watch… *Fox News.*

PROFESSOR: I'm glad you enjoy it that much.

GILBERT: So, I went behind her back…

GREGORY: *Kyle! (beat; change up) Fox News* is *way* more trustworthy than Facebüch!

VIOLA: Professor, did your husband find a job?

PROFESSOR: Actually, he's interviewing for the university right now. Probably.

GILBERT: I was brainstorming a list of potential names because obviously Gilbert Gilbert is a little much.

MALLORY: Obviously.

VIOLA: Ah. Hence the *Hallelujah Chorus*.

PROFESSOR: Jesus– yes.

GILBERT: So, I chose… (*starts a drumroll, is interrupted*)

VIOLA: We're back! (*no one replies*) Okay, *no one* said, "Thank you back," after I said, "We're back." So, let's try that again. (*clears throat*) We're *back*!

ALL: Thank you back.

*Some are enthusiastic, some are annoyed, some are snoring.*

PROFESSOR: Let's get back to 'A Rose for Emily.'

KYLE: Who's Emily?

SFX: LOG ON

*Bri finally joins the class late, just like normal.*

VIOLA: She's a recluse who–

GILBERT: That's me! I'm Emily! I'm changing my name to Emily! Surprise!

BRI: Hey! Hey! Sorry I'm late.

KYLE: Hate to break it to you Gilby, but there are a *lot* of Emily's– Emily Club repre-*sent!*

*Kyle raises a freakin' dope-ass salute in an ASL "E."*

MALLORY: Emily is my Alpha Kappa Fugma sister!

VIOLA: We're back, so could we maybe listen to the lecture now?

GREGORY: Tweetær says anyone named Emily is a carrier of the *plague!*

ZACK: EVERYONE SHUT THE FUCK UP! I'M TRYING TO SLEEP!!!

SFX: LOG OFF

PARTIAL BLACKOUT

*The lights fall to a blackout, except a spotlight on Professor. Her face is a confusing mix of annoyance, joy, acceptance, and... hope.* The Hallelujah Chorus *crescendos, then:*

FULL BLACKOUT

# END OF PLAY

# APPENDIX

## I. PROPERTIES

A variety of nine computers with webcams.

Nine personal cellphones.

Various notebooks, pens, pencils, papers, etc.

A toothbrush.

A coffee cup.

A glass of wine.

A packet of papers. Later, a *thick* packet of papers.

A copy of Jhumpa Lahiri's *A Temporary Matter.*

A Bluetooth speaker.

An edible banana.

Various facemasks. One 'heavy-dutier' than the rest.

A fire extinguisher.

A measuring tape.

A blue rubber glove.

Post-it notes.

A Rubik's Cube.

A calculator.

A large book.

A videogame controller.

A can of Lysol.

A course textbook.

## II. MUSIC REFERENCES

*The Hallelujah Chorus* – G. F. Handel

*Moonlight Sonata*, m. 1 – Ludwig van Beethoven

*The Magic Flute*, "Der Hölle Rache" – W. A. Mozart

*Academic Festival Overture*, op. 80 – Johannes Brahms

## III. NOTES FOR THE DIRECTOR

**COMMUNICATION:** While the play certainly satirizes the use of video conferencing software for education, the main theme discussed here is communication; the hostility and altogether lack-of marital communication, the sterility of corporate communication, and the condescension of educational communication. Technology is both a huge boost and a vast detriment to our communication skills.

**CLASSICAL MUSIC:** The use of classical music is crucial to this story. Firstly, much of technology is seen as 'holier than thou,' and that very idea is brought to light using the *Hallelujah Chorus* as the introduction to the online meeting. Additionally, classical music stands as a clear juxtaposition to the hyper-technological period we find ourselves in; it is meant to help the audience understand the satire.

**FINAL THOUGHTS:** My last note to the director, as well as the cast and creative team: create *your* interpretation of this play. I have many guidelines written into the script, but they are just that: guidelines. They are not rules, and I encourage the actors to make use of improv and ad-libbing and to not strictly follow the written stage directions. I encourage the creative team to reimagine this piece in larger and more nuanced ways than I have, and to find new interpretations that expand on my ideas. After all, this play is not *my* experience, it is a reflection of *our* experience. Work together, take the play to new heights; don't get stuck in a box.

# ABOUT THE AUTHOR

(photo credit: Kelly Tunney)

Caedon Venné is a Pittsburgh-based actor, composer, and playwright. While he is an adept storyteller, *A Temporary Matter* is his debut publication. He recently earned his B.S.ed. in Secondary Education as well as his B.S. in Mathematics at Pennsylvania Western University, California Campus. He is looking to continue his post-baccalaureate education in the realm of theatre to keep the art of storytelling alive through education.

To keep in touch with Caedon, visit
caedonvenne.com
Instagram: @caedon.v